Cook, Eat, Cha Cha Cha

Cook, Eat, Cha Cha Cha

Festive New World Recipes

by Philip Bellber   Photographs by Ian Reeves

CHRONICLE BOOKS

SAN FRANCISCO

Text copyright © 1997 by Philip Bellber.
Photographs copyright © 1997 by Ian Reeves.
All rights reserved. No part of this book may be repro-
duced in any form without written permission from the
publisher.

Library of Congress Cataloging-in-Publication Data:
Bellber, Philip.
      Cook, eat, cha cha cha: festive new world
recipes/by Philip Bellber; photographs by Ian Reeves.
          p. cm.
      Includes bibliographical references and index.
      ISBN 0-8118-1146-8 (pb)
      1. Cookery, Latin American. 2. Cookery, Caribbean.
3. Cookery, American. 4. Restaurants—California—San
Francisco. 5. Santeria. 6. Cha Cha Cha (Restaurant:
San Francisco, Calif.) I. Title.
TX716.A1B45 1997
641.5'09794'61—dc20   96-18698
                                             CIP

Printed in Hong Kong

Designed by: Robin Weiss
Food and Prop Styling by Elizabeth C. Davis

Cha Cha Cha in San Francisco is not affiliated in any
way with any restaurant in Southern California of
the same name.

Distributed in Canada by Raincoast Books
8680 Cambie Street
Vancouver, B.C. V6P 6M9

10 9 8 7 6 5 4 3 2 1

Chronicle Books
85 Second Street
San Francisco, CA 94105

Web Site: www.chronbooks.com

Contents

Introduction

Food always leads to the heart.

Growing up in the fifties in New York City's Spanish Harlem, I spent a lot of time at my grandmother's house. *Abuela* Aya's door was never locked, and I would run up her front stoop and through a maze of hallways to her tiny apartment and into her kitchen. There were always lots of people at Aya's—neighbors, relatives—and as is the Puerto Rican custom, there was always food.

On her stove, Aya kept a pot of hot water, with a pot of meat or chicken on top of it, and on top of that another pot, of *habichuelas quisadas*—rice and beans—and on top of all this, a plate of platanos. This tower of food resembled the *fiambreras*—the white stacked lunchboxes—that Puerto Rican and Cuban workers often take with them into the sugarcane fields.

When someone came into her home, Aya would greet them, "Are you hungry? Do you want something to eat?" That's the way life was then.

And there was always music: cha cha chas, merengues, mambos, and of course, jíbaros, traditional Puerto Rican songs of lost love. Occasionally my uncle would take out his guitar and sing, and at parties, everyone would dance. I danced with Aya, cousins danced with aunts and uncles. Aya's home was very small, six people living in a one-bedroom apartment, but it was always welcoming and full of life.

What seemed ordinary to me then now seems magical. In Aya's apartment, and in the other rooms of my childhood, images of Catholic saints—candles and shrines—abounded. I overlooked them at the time, as part of my everyday landscape, and it was only much later that I recognized some of these Catholic saints as *orishas* of the Santería religion.

Good food, good music, good talk, a little bit of magic: These were the elements of my childhood and are today my most vivid memories. How could I have known then that I would one day, and quite inadvertently, re-create this world in a restaurant in San Francisco?

I've always been at a bit of a loss to describe the food at Cha Cha Cha. Early on, when people would phone the restaurant and ask what type of food we served, instead of trying to categorize our cuisine, I would name the dishes on our menu. Soon, people started to call our food New World cuisine, and the term seemed to fit just fine. Considering the unexpected changes in the restaurant, the eclectic menu, and the wide variety of people involved in its creation, New World cuisine seems appropriate.

When I first met my partner Leon Pak, I thought he had the strangest Chinese accent I'd ever heard. I soon discovered that he was a Habanero; he had moved from China as a child and grew up in Havana. What else would a Chinese Cuban and a first-generation American Puerto Rican from New York do in San Francisco? We bought a pizza parlor on Haight Street.

Fortunately, the pizza parlor didn't pan out, so Leon and I reopened the restaurant as Cha Cha Cha, with a traditional Cuban and Puerto Rican menu: *piñonos, picadillo, lechan asado, bistec encebollado.* Both Leon and I had moved around a great deal as adults, and we each had a soft spot for these childhood foods.

At about this time, I heard about tapas from a cousin of mine in Chicago, and these small dishes seemed to be the perfect addition to our menu, a way of enticing the rather sophisticated palate of San Francisco diners. In Spain, tapas are small plates of appetizers put over your drinks at bars (from the Spanish *tapar,* to cover). Each bar usually has one tapa for which it is known. We made our own version of tapas—larger portions, more ingredients—so that our tapas would be more like small meals, rather than appetizers.

Oftentimes, Leon and I would sit at the bar in the back of the restaurant, sampling the new ideas and creations of our young, dynamic chef, Jimmy Harris. One day Jimmy brought out a dish of spicy Cajun shrimp. It was too spicy at first, like fire; the guy loved hot food. Then it was too bland. Then he hit it right on the head, and we knew it from the first bite.

Somehow, that seems to me like the beginning of Cha Cha Cha.

Soon the menu began to reflect a broader range of Caribbean influences: Jamaican jerk chicken, *yucca al mojo,* spicy chayote salad. We used more fish and shellfish, and began to incorporate fruits and varied spices in our chutneys and sauces. We let our chefs— from all over the world—use their imaginations. Soon we discovered that we had developed an original menu: Cuban and Puerto Rican based, and spiced by Caribbean cooking and the fresh ingredients available to us in California.

Everyone seemed to enjoy it. You could come in with a group of friends, order lots of different and original dishes, drink some sangría, talk, eat, and laugh. But there was still something missing.

In 1988, my wife Rosemary and I visited my relatives in Puerto Rico. My cousin Gloria is a devout Santero, and she showed us the Santería altars in her home, describing the practices and beliefs of her religion. It was on that trip that I came to realize that for much of my life I had been surrounded by the images and rituals of this religion.

Santería is the New World's modification of the ancient Yoruban religion. In the eighteenth and nineteenth centuries, most of the people brought to Cuba as slaves were from Yoruba (what is now called Nigeria), and they brought their beliefs with them.

Forced to worship in secret, the Yoruba, like others in the Americas, adapted their religion to the saints of Catholicism. Each of the Yoruban *orishas*, or *santos* (saints), was identified—syncretized—with a Catholic saint. Babalú-Ayé donned the trappings of St. Lazarus, Changó became St. Barbara, and so on. Over the centuries, though the Yoruban religion was practiced in secret, it spread throughout the New World, to Brazil, Haiti, Trinidad, the United States, and especially to Cuba.

In Cuban Santería, the six hundred deities of the Yoruban religion have been reduced to twenty. Each deity is a direct recipient of the *ashé*, or life force, of Oloddumare, the supreme creator of the universe. In many ways the Santería *orishas* are like the gods of Greek mythology. Each *orisha* is a representation of one of the natural forces and, like the Greek gods, has a personality that is individual and often capricious. The eventual goal of Santería is to find, with the aid of the *orishas*, the harmony in nature and among people, and thereby to enjoy the wonderful adventure of Oloddumare's universe. Santería is a complex and deeply spiritual religion, which I cannot hope to do justice to here, but we have included a bibliography on page 131 to point you to a further understanding of this vital way of life.

When followers are admitted into Santería, they are assigned to a specific *orisha*, to whom they build an altar of devotion. Each day, in every house, Santeros turn to their *orisha* for guidance, offering sacrifices and prayers at their altar. The altar is constructed of fabrics and objects in the colors of the *orisha*, and is furnished with *fundamentos*, those items associated with the *orisha's* powers and appetites. Usually, a votive candle of the Catholic saint identified with the *orisha* is set on the altar as well. A Santero may build altars to other *orishas*, but the altar of the ruling *orisha* is the largest and most beautiful one in the home.

I was enchanted with the altars that Gloria showed us and thought of putting similar ones in the restaurant, but I was afraid of offending followers of Santería. After all, these altars are sacred. Gloria told me that as long as we built the altars with reverence for the *orishas*, there could be no objection. Our altars have become such an integral part of Cha Cha Cha that each chapter of this book is dedicated to one of our *orishas*.

During that same trip to Puerto Rico, I rediscovered the music that I had heard in my childhood, and when I returned home, we broadened the scope of the Caribbean music in the restaurant. We also sought out lots of African music, which was the original inspiration for much of the music I had known as a child. There's a discography on page 130 to help you recreate the perfect Cha Cha Cha meal.

The addition of the Santería altars, along with the new music, seemed to complete the search for Cha Cha Cha's identity. After this, the restaurant seemed to take on a life of its own.

Like a lot of people, life has taken me all over the world, and now I live in a city where almost everyone is from somewhere else. But one day, sitting in Cha Cha Cha, I realized I had come home again. Good food, good music, warm people. The plates of *arroz con pollo*, songs from the mountains of Puerto Rico, the images of saints adorning the walls. To some this is a new experience, to others it's the warm comfort of a shared culture, but for everyone here in San Francisco, it's a new world.

When you join us here at the restaurant, we want you to feel at home. Are you hungry? Do you want something to eat? Come in, sit down, we'll talk. Be comfortable, have a good time.

If you can't visit us, however, here are a few tips on preparing the perfect Cha Cha Cha meal at home.

Don't forget the music. While you are cooking, and while you are serving, we really believe that the right music will enliven your meal. It lets you dance while you cook—music spices up everything—and makes you have to talk a little louder over the meal with your guests, all in celebration.

While we have changed and adapted the original concept of tapas at Cha Cha Cha, we still call all of our dishes by that name, and hope that you'll think of your dinners in the same way, creating a meal of many tastes and textures, much as you would put together a dinner in a Chinese restaurant. Depending on how many guests you will serve, choose some of your favorite dishes and a few you're trying for the first time, then put them all together.

Although there are no true courses in a Cha Cha Cha meal, our first chapter is dedicated to openers, those lighter dishes we use to start the meal, awaken the taste buds, and get everyone talking. The serving portions given for our openers are smaller, then, than the dishes in the later chapters, where the portions are slightly bigger. As a rule of thumb, we suggest one tapa for each guest, but we leave the choices up to you. There are no rules for a Cha Cha Cha meal, just lots of good food. Always make a little too much food, and be creative. Sangría, dark beer, fresh fruit juices, and bottled waters are the perfect beverages for our food. And don't forget to end the meal with a Cuban-style coffee, dark and strong, with lots of sugar.

Before your guests arrive, light a candle (or several), say a prayer to the four corners, and open your door with gracious arms. This is not simply food, it's a celebration. *Mi casa es su casa.*

Chapter One

Ellegua

SOUPS, OPENERS, AND SALADS

Ellegua is the first of all the *orishas*, Oloddumare's messenger and the keeper of the gate between the worlds. Every Santería ceremony begins with a song of praise and offerings to Ellegua. If you forget to bow to Ellegua, then his trickster self, Eshú, may appear in your life, spreading chaos.

Ellegua is the overseer of all earthly passages as well, all beginnings and endings. He lives in every place of passage: in the hospital, in the church, in the four corners of the block, in the garbage, in the cemeteries, across the river, in the forest. Offerings to Ellegua (often a coconut) are found behind nearly every door in a Santero home.

Lurking in every doorway, Ellegua is the watcher of all human actions, and the judge of those actions. In Brazil, where he is called Exu, he has been identified with the Christian devil because of his harsh judgments and the chaos he can deliver. But in Cuba, he has been identified with St. Anthony, the miracle worker, and he is identified with fate or destiny. He brings great joy or great sorrow. In this dual nature, he acts as a champion of justice, swiftly punishing the wicked and rewarding the virtuous.

Ellegua is also a warrior. His colors are red and black (Eshú, his trickster self, employs black and white). He has twenty-one aspects; his numbers are three, seven, and twenty-one. Monday is his day of worship. Ellegua's favorite offerings are cookies and sweets, toys, popcorn, rum, and tobacco. His emblem is the hooked staff, which allows him to clear a path through the difficult ways of the jungle. When Ellegua dances, he assumes the movement of the buffoon or the clown.

Here is the traditional invocation to Ellegua, which you may want to use at the beginning of your meal:

> *Laroye, akiloye, agurotenteonu*
> *Apagura, acamasese*
> *Okoloofofo, okolonini, tonicanofo, omo orogun, ollona alayiki*
> *Ayuba*

And don't forget, when your meal is finished, leave a bowl of scraps outside your door for Eshú, the trickster Ellegua. This should keep him satisfied, unable to visit his chaos upon your home.

Fish Stock

Makes 3 to 4 quarts

Fish stock is the basis for many soups and sauces. Halibut bones make the best fish stocks; they are not fatty and their flavor is quite subtle. Other fish bones that work well are those of snapper, rock cod, sole, and sea bass. If you don't have time to make the fish stock, we recommend canned clam juice as a substitute.

3 to 4 pounds halibut bones and trimmings

2 to 3 celery stalks, coarsely chopped

1 carrot, coarsely chopped

½ large onion

4 bay leaves

10 black peppercorns

1 unpeeled garlic head, halved crosswise

2 to 3 tomatoes, coarsely chopped

½ bunch fresh parsley, stemmed and coarsely chopped

1 bunch fresh thyme, or 2 tablespoons dried thyme

Put the halibut bones and trimmings in a stockpot and add water to cover by 6 inches. Place over high heat and, just before the water boils, skim off any scum.

Add all the remaining ingredients and simmer for 1½ hours, periodically skimming the surface.

Strain through a fine-meshed sieve and let cool to room temperature. Cover and refrigerate for up to 3 days. For longer storage, bring to a boil every 3 days, or freeze for up to 3 months.

Chicken Stock

There's nothing quite like homemade chicken stock. If you don't have time to make this stock, we recommend canned low-salt chicken broth as a substitute.

2 to 2½ pounds bony chicken pieces, preferably backs

2 celery stalks, cut into ½-inch dice

2 carrots, peeled and cut into ½-inch dice

1 onion, cut into ½-inch dice

3 to 4 quarts water

6 garlic cloves, crushed

2 bay leaves

1 tablespoon black peppercorns

6 fresh parsley sprigs

6 fresh thyme sprigs

Place the chicken and vegetables in a stockpot and add the water. Bring to a boil, then reduce to a simmer, skimming off the scum that rises to the top.

Add the garlic, bay leaves, peppercorns, parsley, and thyme, and continue cooking for 1½ to 2 hours, skimming occasionally.

Strain and refrigerate. Discard the congealed fat on the top. Cover and store in the refrigerator for up to 3 days. To keep longer, bring to a boil every 3 days, or freeze for up to 3 months.

Cuban Bean Soup

Serves 6 to 8

Served with sourdough bread, this hearty soup is a meal in itself. Ask your butcher for small and meaty smoked ham hocks, as their flavor is stronger and they are easier to handle than the larger ones.

A cook's trick in Cuba these days (due to the lack of meat) is to use roasted bell peppers instead of the ham hocks. These impart a smoky flavor to the soup, and make a nice substitute for vegetarians.

2 to 2½ pounds smoked ham hocks

5 to 6 quarts water

1 pound (2 cups) dried garbanzo beans

1½ onions, coarsely chopped

2 carrots, peeled and coarsely chopped

2 celery stalks, coarsely chopped

½ cabbage head, coarsely chopped

2 unpeeled russet potatoes, coarsely chopped

7 garlic cloves

3 bay leaves

1 cup sofrito (page 34)

Salt and freshly ground pepper to taste

Put the ham hocks and water in a heavy stockpot. Bring to a boil, reduce heat to a slow boil, and cook for 20 to 25 minutes.

Rinse and pick over the garbanzo beans to remove any stones. Add the garbanzo beans to the stockpot and cook for 20 to 25 minutes.

Add the onions, carrots, celery, cabbage, potatoes, garlic, and bay leaves and cook for about 1 to 1½ hours, or until the ham falls from the bone.

Transfer the ham hocks to a plate. Remove and discard the skin and bones. Cut the meat into ¼-inch pieces and return it to the soup.

Add the sofrito, salt, and pepper. Reduce the heat and simmer for 20 to 25 minutes. Taste and adjust the seasoning as necessary.

Grilled-Tomato Gazpacho

Serves 6 to 8

Gazpacho is a wonderful midsummer chilled soup. Because of the cool summer nights in San Francisco, we generally serve our gazpacho for lunch. Gazpacho is also lovely on late September and early October evenings during our Indian Summer.

½ **green bell pepper, halved, seeded, and deveined**

½ **red bell pepper, halved, seeded, and deveined**

2 cucumbers, peeled, halved lengthwise, and seeded

5 large vine-ripened tomatoes, halved

½ **onion, quartered**

½ **teaspoon minced canned chipotle chili**

2 to 3 teaspoons extra-virgin olive oil

3 tablespoons balsamic vinegar

2 teaspoons chopped garlic

¼ **cup minced mixed chopped fresh herbs, such as cilantro, thyme, and parsley**

Salt and freshly ground black pepper to taste

6 to 8 fresh cilantro sprigs

½ **lime**

Light a fire in a charcoal or gas grill. Cut a 1-inch strip from each pepper and cut 1 cucumber half in half crosswise. Finely chop the pepper strips and cucumber half together and reserve for garnish.

Over a medium-hot fire, grill the tomatoes, remaining pepper and cucumbers, and the onion. The tomatoes will be done in 3 to 5 minutes; the peppers, cucumbers, and onion in 7 to 10 minutes.

Place the grilled vegetables, chipotle, oil, vinegar, garlic, and chopped herbs in a blender or food processor and blend to a smooth paste. Add the salt and pepper, cover, and refrigerate for at least 1 or 2 hours, or place in the freezer until very cold.

To serve, pour the gazpacho into chilled shallow soup bowls. Sprinkle with the reserved chopped vegetables. Garnish each serving with a cilantro sprig and a splash of freshly squeezed lime.

Fried Plantains

Serves 6

Our most popular appetizer is fried plantains served over black bean puree, all drizzled with a little (or a lot) of sour cream. Make sure the plantains are ripe; the skin should be almost completely black. Fried plantains are also great served by themselves.

1½ cups vegetable oil

3 ripe plantains, peeled and cut into 2-inch diagonal slices

2 cups cooked black beans, drained (page 61)

⅓ cup sour cream

In a large, heavy skillet over medium heat, heat the oil until it is fragrant and fry the plantains for 4 to 6 minutes, or until they are a dark golden brown. Using a slotted spoon, transfer them to paper towels to drain.

Puree the beans in a blender or food processor, adding some broth from the beans if the puree is too thick.

Make a bed of puree on each of 6 small plates and top with the plantains. Drizzle with the sour cream. Serve warm.

Sautéed Mushrooms

Serves 3 to 5

This Cha Cha Cha classic is easy to prepare in any kitchen, and goes well with grilled meats and fish. The combination of garlic, sherry, and butter keeps our customers dunking sourdough bread in the juice all through their meal.

4 tablespoons olive oil

18 to 22 white mushrooms, stemmed

1 tablespoon minced garlic

⅓ teaspoon dried basil

⅓ teaspoon dried thyme

⅓ teaspoon dried oregano

2 scallions, finely chopped, white part only

Pinch of red pepper flakes

½ cup dry sherry

4 tablespoons unsalted butter, cut into pieces

Salt and freshly ground pepper to taste

In a large, heavy skillet over medium-high heat, heat 2 tablespoons of the oil until it smokes. Add the mushroom caps and sauté for 1 to 2 minutes, stirring constantly.

Add the remaining 2 tablespoons olive oil, the garlic, herbs, scallions, and pepper flakes, and sauté for 1 to 2 minutes. Add the sherry and cook to reduce it by half. Swirl in the butter a little at a time to glaze the mushrooms. Add salt and pepper. Serve immediately.

Christine's Vegetable Empanadas

Makes 6
empanadas

Traditionally, these turnovers are filled with finely chopped beef, olives, and capers. At Cha Cha Cha we make ours with the bountiful vegetables available year round in California. We have also used shrimp, chicken, and pork. The best part of making this dish is inventing new fillings.

2 cups unbleached all-purpose flour

2 cups corn flour

½ teaspoon salt

¼ teaspoon sugar

1 teaspoon dried basil

1 teaspoon baking powder

⅔ cup (1⅓ sticks) cold unsalted butter, cut into pieces

1¼ cups ice water

VEGETABLE FILLING

¼ cup vegetable oil

½ red bell pepper, seeded, deveined, and cut into ¼-inch dice

¼ yellow onion, cut into ¼-inch dice

1 cup ¼-inch-diced eggplant

2 celery stalks, cut into ¼-inch dice

½ cup fresh or frozen corn kernels (1 ear)

1 teaspoon minced garlic

½ teaspoon ground cumin

½ teaspoon red pepper flakes

Salt and freshly ground black pepper to taste

1 cup (4 ounces) grated Monterey jack or smoked Gouda cheese

2 eggs, beaten

¼ cup vegetable oil for frying (optional)

Creole Sauce (page 46)

Place the flours, salt, sugar, basil, and baking powder in a food processor and cut the butter in for 3 to 5 minutes, or until the mixture looks like cornmeal. Slowly add the ice water and pulse until the mixture forms a ball.

Or, to make by hand, combine the dry ingredients in a large bowl and cut in the butter with a pastry cutter or 2 knives. Sprinkle with the ice water and mix with a fork. Form into a ball with your hands. Cover and refrigerate while making the vegetable filling.

To make the vegetable filling: In a medium skillet over medium-high heat, heat the oil and sauté the vegetables for 2 to 3 minutes, or until the onion is translucent. Add the garlic, cumin, pepper flakes, salt, and pepper. Sauté for 2 to 3 minutes. Using a slotted spoon, transfer to paper towels to drain.

Place the dough on a lightly floured surface and roll out to a ⅛-inch thickness. Cut out six 6½-inch circles, rerolling the scraps as necessary.

Place one sixth of the cheese and the vegetable filling in the center of each circle. Brush the edges of each circle with the beaten egg wash, fold the circle in half, and seal with your fingers or a fork.

Gently brush each empanada with beaten egg. In a large, heavy pot or deep-fryer, heat 3 inches of oil over medium-high heat to 350°F, or until fragrant. Fry the empanadas until golden brown, about 3 to 5 minutes. Using a slotted spoon, transfer them to paper towels to drain. Or, bake in a preheated 375°F oven for 12 to 15 minutes, or until golden brown. Serve warm, with Creole Sauce.

Spicy Guacamole

The key to this recipe is the jalapeños. If the chilies come from Mexico, they will be hot; from the south of Mexico, very hot. No matter the country of origin, the flavor of the jalapeño is always rich and savory. But, hey, it should be a little too hot. Serve this with tortilla chips as an appetizer, or as a sauce with grilled fish or chicken, or with tortilla dishes.

5 ripe avocados, peeled and pitted

½ bunch fresh cilantro, stemmed and minced

1 tomato, finely diced

1 onion, finely chopped

⅓ cup fresh lemon juice

2 teaspoons salt

1 teaspoon ground white pepper

3 jalapeño chilies, seeded and minced

1 teaspoon habanero or Tabasco sauce

Place the avocados in a large bowl and mash them to the desired consistency. Blend in all the remaining ingredients. Store in an airtight container in the refrigerator for up to 1 week.

Warm Spinach Salad

Serves 4 to 6

A variation of this rustic country-style salad evolved one night at Cha Cha Cha when a customer wanted his spinach chopped into smaller pieces (I don't know why he didn't use his knife and fork), and a perfectly lovely salad reappeared in front of chef Vinnie Wright, who in his inimitable New York accent said, "He wants it smaller, huh?" and put the salad in a blender. Back to the customer it went, looking for all the world like something out of a Gerber's jar. However, the customer thought it was just right. "Go figure," as Vinnie would say.

2 bunches spinach, stemmed

6 bacon slices

1 bunch scallions, cut into ¼-inch pieces, including some green tops

10 white mushrooms, thinly sliced

¼ cup dry sherry

½ recipe Dijon Mustard Sauce (page 77)

2 tablespoons chopped fresh parsley

2 tablespoons chopped fresh cilantro

Salt and freshly ground black pepper to taste

1 cup (4 ounces) grated Parmesan cheese

Wash and dry the spinach, and place it in a large bowl. Set aside.

In a large, heavy skillet over medium heat, brown the bacon lightly. Using tongs, transfer the bacon to paper towels to drain. Crumble the bacon into bits. Pour off all but 2 tablespoons of bacon fat.

In the same skillet over medium heat, cook the scallions and mushrooms for 2 minutes, or until lightly browned. Add the sherry, stir to scrape the browned bits from the bottom of the pan, and cook over medium heat to reduce the liquid by half. Add the mustard sauce, parsley, cilantro, salt, and pepper.

Pour this mixture over the spinach, gently toss with Parmesan cheese, and add the bacon bits. Serve immediately.

Spicy Cabbage Salad

Serves 4 to 6

This salad goes wonderfully well with grilled rib-eye steak, duck, skirt steak, and duck breast. It can be prepared the night before and keeps for about a week in the refrigerator. Like ourselves, this salad seems to get better with age.

Although this dish was originally brought to us from Costa Rica by Gabby Salas, this version is Andrew Gillen's, and is as subtle and savory as the original.

2 cups jalapeño-flavored vinegar

¾ cup sugar

1 tablespoon habanero or Tabasco sauce

Dash of salt

1 cup fresh lemon juice

2½ teaspoons toasted sesame oil

1 red cabbage, cored and shredded

1 green cabbage, cored and shredded

4 carrots, peeled and shredded

1 bunch fresh cilantro, stemmed and minced

In a large bowl, combine the vinegar and sugar. Whisk vigorously while adding the habanero or Tabasco sauce, salt, lemon juice, and sesame oil.

Add the cabbage, carrots, and cilantro, and toss. Let sit at room temperature for 1 hour before serving. To store, cover and refrigerate for up to 1 week.

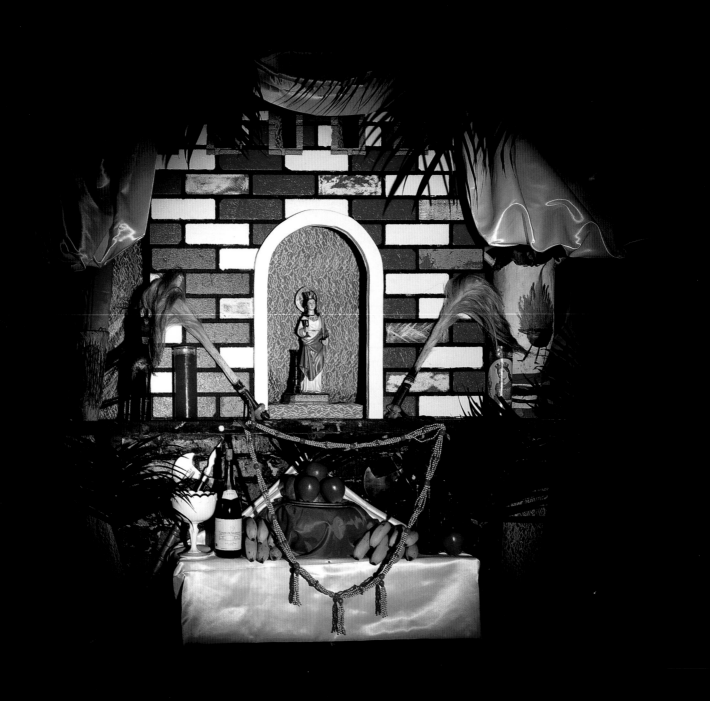

Chapter Two

Changó

SAUCES AND SPICES

Changó is the Adonis of Santería, the handsome warrior who represents the essence of male sexuality. He is the custodian of fire, thunder, and lightning, and of the drums. His is the energy behind the raucous parties that are so much a part of Santerían and Cuban life. When the song of Changó begins, you have no choice but to dance. He has had many wives (Oyá, Oshún, and Obba), and he tends to be suspicious and jealous of his sons. He covets the gold and riches of others, especially those of the bridal dowry.

It is Changó's driving passion that brings forth the rains that feed both the rivers and the oceans; at the same time he is often seen as fire, which evaporates the life-giving water. In Changó's dualism, we can see that passion and virility must be held in balance, so that a forceful and orderly life can be lived. With such a balance, enemies and obstacles can be wisely overcome. Devout followers of Changó are protected by his great warlike fierceness.

Changó's passion is not only romantic and sexual, but is often the inspiration for artists, musicians, and writers.

Simply put, Changó is the spice of life. Too much and you will be burned; not enough and life is dull. Just the right amount of spice is needed in the Santería cosmology.

Changó's colors are red and white. His numbers are four and six, and his day of the week is Friday. He has been syncretized with St. Barbara. His favorite offerings are bananas and farina, but he is also fond of rooster, sheep, goat, pig, and of course, bull. The symbol most frequently found on Changó's red and white altar is the *oshé*, the warrior's double-headed axe. The dance of Changó is a frenzied flight of acrobatics.

Roasted-Beet Vinaigrette

Makes 2 cups

This and the following vinaigrettes are fast, relatively low in fat, and flavorful. Enjoy them on baby lettuces, and with grilled chicken and fish.

2 beets (about 8 ounces total)

3 tablespoons red wine vinegar

1 tablespoon Dijon mustard

2 tablespoons fresh lemon juice

1 tablespoon minced onion

2 tablespoons minced mixed fresh cilantro, chives, and parsley

1 cup vegetable oil

Salt and freshly ground pepper to taste

Preheat oven to 350°F. Wrap each beet in aluminum foil, place in a baking dish, and bake for 45 to 60 minutes, or until tender. Let cool, peel, and cut into pieces.

Place the beets and all the remaining ingredients, except the oil, salt, and pepper, in a blender or food processor and puree. With the machine running, drizzle the oil into the mixture. Add the salt and pepper. Store in an airtight container in the refrigerator for up to 3 weeks.

Mango Vinaigrette

Makes 2 cups

1 mango, peeled

Grated zest and juice of 1 lime

1 tablespoon chopped fresh cilantro

1 teaspoon sugar

⅓ cup seasoned rice wine vinegar

1 teaspoon honey mustard

1 cup vegetable oil or light olive oil

Salt and freshly ground black pepper to taste

Cut the mango flesh away from the pit and chop the mango coarsely. Place the mango and all the remaining ingredients, except the oil, salt, and pepper, in a blender or food processor and puree. With the machine running, drizzle in the oil. Add the salt and pepper. Store in an airtight container in the refrigerator for up to 3 weeks.

Coco Vinaigrette

Makes 1½ cups

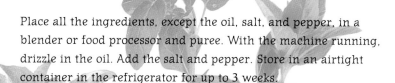

1½ **tablespoons minced fresh oregano, or ½ tablespoon dried**

1½ **tablespoons minced fresh basil**

¼ **cup red wine vinegar**

2 **tablespoons fresh lemon juice**

1 **teaspoon minced garlic**

1 **tablespoon Dijon mustard**

1 **teaspoon capers, drained**

1 **teaspoon sugar**

¼ **cup coconut milk**

3 **scallions, finely chopped, including some green tops**

¾ **cup vegetable oil**

Salt and freshly ground black pepper to taste

Place all the ingredients, except the oil, salt, and pepper, in a blender or food processor and puree. With the machine running, drizzle in the oil. Add the salt and pepper. Store in an airtight container in the refrigerator for up to 3 weeks.

Sofrito

Sofrito is a spicy sauce that is stirred into certain dishes, primarily beans, during the last stages of cooking and mixed thoroughly into the beans. It's the one ingredient that turns a bowl of plain beans into a meal.

My business partner Leon Pak and his wife Isabel spent most of their lives in Cuba, but they are originally from China, and the way Isabel fries her sofrito, fast over high heat, is almost like stir-frying. Her sofrito gives her bean soups (both black and red) a smoky, sweet flavor. This is a comfort food that would make anyone feel at home anywhere in the world.

3 tablespoons olive oil

2 green bell peppers, seeded, deveined, and cut into ½-inch dice

1 red bell pepper, seeded, deveined, and cut into ½-inch dice

1½ onions, cut into ½-inch dice

2 tomatoes, coarsely chopped

2 teaspoons dried oregano

1 teaspoon ground cumin or to taste

2 tablespoons minced garlic

½ bunch fresh parsley, stemmed and minced

¼ cup vinegar

½ cup dry white wine

In a large, heavy 12-inch skillet over high heat, heat the olive oil and sauté the peppers and onions for 3 to 4 minutes, or until the onions are translucent. Reduce heat to low, add the remaining ingredients, and simmer for 4 to 5 minutes, or until the vegetables are tender. Store in an airtight container in the refrigerator for up to 3 weeks.

Cajun Spice Mix

Makes 1⅓ cups

Jimmy Harris cooked at Cha Cha Cha from the very beginning, just about the same time that the Cajun craze was sweeping the country. I can still see him with smoke billowing around his head (there was no way our original undersized exhaust hood could handle this Cajun thing), his eyes smarting and a look of utter satisfaction on his face. It was at his urging that we first blackened some of our dishes, and smoke or no smoke, he was elated with his success. Our customers threw back huge pitchers of water and sangria to put out the fires he'd started.

Use this spice mix in Blackening Spices (page 37), Skillet Cajun Shrimp (page 107), and Salmon Croquettes with Tomato Coulis (page 102), and to create your own Cajun dishes.

½ cup sweet paprika

2½ tablespoons cayenne pepper

2½ tablespoons garlic powder

2½ tablespoons onion powder

1½ tablespoons ground black pepper

1½ tablespoons ground white pepper

1 tablespoon dried thyme

1 tablespoon dried oregano

1 tablespoon salt

Combine all the ingredients and mix well. Store in an airtight container in a cool, dry place.

Blackening Spices

Makes 6
tablespoons

This fiery spice combo can be used to cook meats and poultry, but is especially good with fish. We use it on our snapper, salmon, and grouper. For the proper blackening technique, refer to the method for Blackened Pacific Salmon Quesadillas (page 104).

When blackening anything, be sure to cook in a well-ventilated area, and make every attempt not to inhale the smoke from the skillet.

¼ cup Cajun Spice Mix (page 35)
1 tablespoon sweet paprika
1 tablespoon ground cumin

Combine all the ingredients and mix well. Store in an airtight container in a cool, dry place.

Salsa Fresca

Makes 4 cups

Salsa and chips are always waiting at your table when you visit Cha Cha Cha. They wake up your taste buds and enliven all your senses for the meal to come. A touch more or less of jalapeño changes the salsa dramatically. Like everything at Cha Cha Cha, our salsa evolves continually, especially when our prep person is from Mexico—here comes that touch more of jalapeño! Serve this with tortilla chips, quesadillas, or fried foods.

12 tomatoes, quartered

1 green bell pepper, seeded, deveined, and chopped

2 tablespoons chopped fresh cilantro

½ onion, chopped

4 canned jalapeño chilies, or 2 fresh jalapeños, seeded and chopped

¼ teaspoon salt

Cracked black pepper to taste

Place all the ingredients in a blender or food processor and pulse for 1 to 2 minutes, or to the desired consistency. Store in an airtight container in the refrigerator for up to 2 weeks.

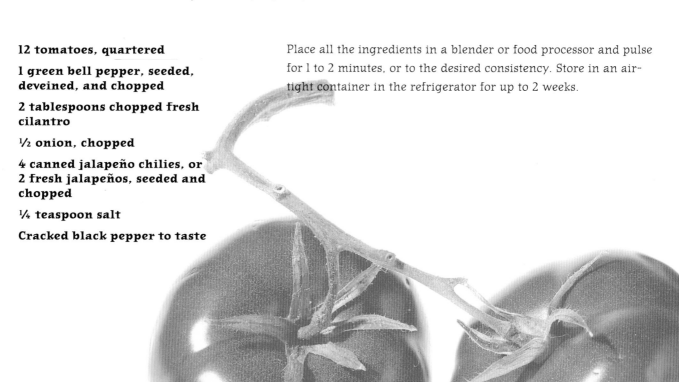

Gabriela's Banana Salsa

Makes 1½ cups

Gabby is a great interpreter of our food, and her addition of rice wine vinegar to this salsa, which gives it an unexpected Asian tang, is exactly the kind of inspiration that has made Cha Cha Cha what it is today. Banana salsa goes well with Snapper in Banana Leaves (page 100) and all fresh fish.

½ **cup mashed banana (about 1 banana)**

1 cup coconut milk

¼ **cup seasoned rice wine vinegar**

1 teaspoon minced garlic

2 tablespoons minced fresh cilantro

1 tablespoon honey (optional)

1 cup olive or canola oil

Salt and freshly ground black pepper to taste

Place all the ingredients, except the oil, salt, and pepper, in a blender or food processor and puree to a thick paste.

With the machine running, slowly drizzle the oil into the mixture to make a creamy salsa. If the salsa appears too thick, thin it with a couple of drops of cold water. Add salt and pepper.

Store in the refrigerator, tightly covered, for up to 5 days.

Lemon Aioli

To me, Spicy Fried Calamari (page 99) and lemon aioli are a perfect combination. If you can't or won't try this duo at home, come on down to the restaurant with your copy of this book, and we'll make you up a batch—for free! Lemon aioli is also a wonderful accompaniment to raw vegetables, and it can spruce up any sandwich.

Grated zest and juice of 3 lemons

1½ tablespoons Dijon mustard

1 tablespoon minced garlic

2 egg yolks

½ tablespoon ground white pepper

½ teaspoon salt

1½ slices white bread, crusts removed and bread torn into pieces

2 cups olive or canola oil

½ cup of ice water (optional)

Place the zest, juice, mustard, garlic, egg yolks, pepper, salt, and bread in a blender or food processor and puree to a smooth paste.

With the machine running, drizzle in the oil. If the aioli appears too thick, add 2 tablespoons of water at a time to adjust the consistency. Store in an airtight jar in the refrigerator for up to 2 weeks.

Pasilla Aioli

Makes 3½ to 4 cups

Pasilla chili paste adds a unique flavor and color to this aioli. It goes well with grilled or fried vegetables, and sautéed or baked seafood.

4 pasilla chilies, seeded

3 tablespoons pasilla powder

2 tablespoons olive oil

2 egg yolk

1½ slices white bread, crusts removed, soaked in ¼ cup red wine vinegar

¼ cup Dijon mustard

1 teaspoon salt

¼ teaspoon ground white pepper

2 teaspoons minced garlic

1 tablespoon fresh lemon juice

3 cups soybean oil

freshly ground pepper to taste

In a medium saucepan of boiling water, blanch the chilies for 2 minutes. Drain, reserving ⅓ cup of the water. In a blender or food processor, combine the water, blanched chilies, pasilla powder, and olive oil, and puree to a smooth paste.

Add all the remaining ingredients, except for the soybean oil, and puree. With the machine running, drizzle in the soybean oil. Store in an airtight container in the refrigerator for up to 10 days.

Orange-Chipotle Hollandaise

Makes 1½ cups

We serve this sauce with our Sunday brunches. It goes great with poached eggs on jalapeño Cheese Corn Bread (page 57), and is unexpectedly good with grilled fish and meats.

5 egg yolks

Grated zest of 1 orange

Juice of 2 oranges

3 canned chipotle chilies, pureed

2 to 4 tablespoons dry white wine

1 tablespoon fresh lemon juice

1 cup clarified butter (see page 132)

2 tablespoons minced fresh cilantro

2 tablespoons finely chopped scallions, including some green tops

In a double boiler, combine the egg yolks, orange zest, orange juice, chipotle puree, white wine, and lemon juice. Place over simmering water and whisk until the mixture is frothy and opaque. If the eggs begin to lump at any point, immediately remove them from the heat, dip the bottom of the pan in cold water, and whisk to cool them.

Whisking quickly in a circular motion, slowly add one third of the clarified butter. Continue whisking, adding another third of the butter, and finally the last third. Whisk constantly until all the butter is absorbed and the sauce is thick. Add the herbs. Remove from heat and keep warm over lukewarm water until serving.

Island Barbecue Sauce

Makes 6 to 8 cups

There's nothing like homemade, and this sauce proves it. Use it with ribs, chicken, and duck, as you would your regular bottled brand. At Cha Cha Cha, it complements our sandwiches and quesadillas.

¼ cup olive oil

1 cup finely chopped onions

5 ancho chilies, seeded

2 pasilla chilies, seeded

2 tablespoons minced fresh cilantro

1 tablespoon minced garlic

1 tablespoon ground cumin

1 tablespoon dried thyme

1 tablespoon dried basil

½ cup dark beer

¼ cup distilled white vinegar

1 cup chicken stock (page 14) or canned low-salt chicken broth

¼ cup soy sauce

½ cup fresh lemon juice

¼ cup Dijon mustard

¼ cup Worcestershire sauce

½ cup molasses

2 cups ketchup

2 tomatoes, finely diced

In a large, heavy saucepan over medium heat, heat the olive oil and sauté the onions, chilies, cilantro, garlic, cumin, thyme, and basil until the onions are translucent, 3 to 4 minutes.

Add the beer, vinegar, stock, soy sauce, lemon juice, mustard, Worcestershire sauce, and molasses. Cook to reduce by half.

Add the ketchup and tomatoes. Simmer for 1 hour, or until the chilies are soft. Puree the mixture in a blender or food processor, in batches if necessary. Store tightly covered in the refrigerator for up to 3 weeks.

Creole Sauce

Makes 4 cups *This is the perfect topping for Black Bean Cakes (page 62) and Christine's Vegetable Empanadas (page 22). This sauce is also good over chicken, polenta, and eggs.*

¼ cup olive oil

1½ onions, cut into ½-inch dice

1 green bell pepper, seeded, deveined, and cut into ½-inch dice

1 red bell pepper, seeded, deveined, and cut into ½-inch dice

3 to 4 celery stalks, cut into ½-inch dice

1 tablespoon minced garlic

1 jalapeño chili, seeded and minced

3 to 4 tomatoes, diced, or 3 cups diced canned tomatoes

1 tablespoon unpacked brown sugar

½ cup minced fresh parsley

1 teaspoon Worcestershire sauce

½ teaspoon habanero or Tabasco sauce

½ teaspoon dried basil

½ teaspoon dried thyme

Pinch of cayenne pepper

2 bay leaves

2 teaspoons fresh lemon juice

½ cup golden raisins (optional)

½ cup fresh or frozen corn kernels (about 1 ear), optional

Tomato juice to taste

Salt to taste

In a large saucepan over medium heat, heat the olive oil and sauté the onions, peppers, celery, garlic, and jalapeño for 4 to 6 minutes, or until the onions are translucent. Add the diced tomatoes and brown sugar. Sauté for 3 to 4 minutes, or until the sugar dissolves.

Reduce heat to a simmer and add all the remaining ingredients except the tomato juice and salt. Cook for 10 to 12 minutes, stirring occasionally. Adjust the thickness of the sauce with tomato juice. Season with salt. Serve warm.

Spicy Mango Chutney

Makes 2 cups

Chutney that is properly stored will keep several days, and the fruit and spice flavors will become more intense. We usually serve our chutney over grilled meats or fish, but the cook staff at Cha Cha Cha can often be seen spreading it on bagels during the morning prep, a novel idea for your Sunday brunch.

1 mango, peeled

1 teaspoon unsalted butter

2 tablespoons finely chopped red onion

½ teaspoon minced jalapeño chili

1 teaspoon minced fresh ginger

2 tablespoons red wine vinegar

1 tablespoon packed brown sugar

1 teaspoon ground cumin

1 tablespoon honey

Grated zest of 1 orange

½ cup fresh orange juice

2 tablespoons minced fresh cilantro

1 tablespoon finely chopped red bell pepper

Salt and freshly ground black pepper to taste

Cut the mango flesh away from the pit and cut the flesh into ½-inch dice. Set aside.

In a medium saucepan, melt the butter over medium heat and sauté the onion and jalapeño until the onion is translucent, 1 or 2 minutes.

Add the ginger, vinegar, brown sugar, cumin, honey, orange zest, and orange juice. Continue cooking over medium heat to reduce the mixture by half.

Reduce heat to low and gently stir in the diced mango, cilantro, and bell pepper. Add salt and pepper. Let cool to room temperature and refrigerate for up to 6 days.

Chapter Three

Babalú-Ayé

VEGETABLES AND GRAINS

abalú-Ayé is the patron saint of the infirm and those suffering from illness. He was quickly and aptly matched with Saint Lazarus, and like the Christian martyr, he takes upon himself the illnesses of others in order to cure them. Babalú-Ayé himself is revitalized and cured by the prayers and offerings given up to him. Within Santería, he is the most respected of the saints. He is also a great magician. Everyone, it is certain, will have to turn to Babalú-Ayé sooner or later. He cares for one and all.

Babalú-Ayé is the only *orisha* not originally from the Yoruban religion. He is of the Arara, who were enslaved in Cuba along with the Yoruba. In their new country, under very harsh living conditions, both peoples found the magic and healing powers of Babalú-Ayé an urgent necessity.

At the beginning of the ritual that praises him, Babalú-Ayé crawls across the floor, unable to dance. As the power of the singing and the music reaches him, he begins to rise up and dance, cleansed and ready once again to bring his healing magic to the world.

Babalú-Ayé's colors are lavender, black, and beige. His numbers are thirteen and seventeen, and his day of the week is Friday. To appeal to his good wishes, his followers offer raw beans, rice, and grains, along with small pieces of bread. Like St. Lazarus, he dresses in the sackcloth of the beggar, which often adorns his altar, along with crutches, reeds, and cowrie shells. His dance ends in a stirring testament to the forces of music, prayer, and the basic foods of life.

Roasted-Garlic Sweet Potatoes

Serves 4 to 6   *Serve these with Grilled Pork Chops (page 94) and Mango Chutney (page 47).*

6 small sweet potatoes (about 3 pounds), peeled and cut into large pieces

6 roasted garlic cloves (see Note)

3 tablespoons unsalted butter

½ cup heavy cream, warmed

Cook the sweet potatoes in a large pot of salted boiling water until tender, about 12 to 15 minutes. Drain and mash the potatoes in the pot with the garlic, butter, and cream. Serve warm.

Note: To roast garlic, preheat the oven to 375°F. Cut off the top of one bulb of garlic about ½ inch into the bulb so that the top of each clove is exposed. Brush the bulb with olive oil and sprinkle with salt and pepper. Line a small baking dish with aluminum foil, add the garlic, and bake for 20 to 25 minutes, or until the garlic skin is dark brown. Let cool to room temperature. Separate and peel the cloves.

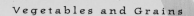

Red Polenta

Serves 6 to 8

Polenta is the "starch king" at Cha Cha Cha. It's so versatile you can eat it for breakfast, for lunch with sautéed vegetables, or grilled for dinner with beef or seafood. Chicken stock can be substituted in place of the water to add more flavor. At Cha Cha Cha we use water, because this dish is frequently used to enhance our vegetarian dishes. Once cooled, the polenta can be covered and stored for 2 to 3 days in the refrigerator.

5 tablespoons unsalted butter

1 cup finely chopped onion

½ red bell pepper, seeded, deveined, and finely chopped

¼ green bell pepper, seeded, deveined, and finely chopped

6 cups water

1½ tablespoon salt

¼ teaspoon ground white pepper

1½ cups polenta

¼ cup minced fresh cilantro

¼ cup minced fresh basil

¼ cup minced fresh chives

In a large, heavy saucepan, melt 1 tablespoon of the butter and cook the onion and bell peppers until the onion is translucent, about 1 to 2 minutes. Add the water, salt, pepper, and the remaining 4 tablespoons of butter. Bring to a boil, then gradually stir in the polenta with a wire whisk.

Reduce heat to medium low and cook the polenta for 25 to 30 minutes, stirring frequently.

When the polenta is fluffy and thick, stir in the cilantro, basil, and chives. Pour the polenta into a lightly oiled 8-inch square baking dish. Let cool to room temperature, then cut into desired shapes.

Zucchini Pancakes with Onions Provençal

Makes 8 pancakes; serves 4

This is a wonderful dish to prepare in the summer when zucchini is at its peak, and it makes a great vegetarian tapa. If the zucchini are large, be sure to remove the center pulp and seeds.

2 eggs

½ cup milk

3 to 4 zucchini, shredded

3 teaspoons minced garlic

⅓ cup each minced fresh parsley, thyme, and basil

½ cup (2 ounces) shredded jalapeño jack cheese (optional)

Pinch of cayenne pepper

½ cup dried bread crumbs

¼ cup unbleached flour

Salt and freshly ground black pepper to taste

4 tablespoons unsalted butter

Onions Provençal (following)

Preheat oven to 250°F. In a large bowl, whisk the egg and milk together. Stir in the shredded zucchini, garlic, herbs, cheese, and cayenne pepper. Slowly add the bread crumbs and flour to the mixture. Add the salt and pepper.

In a large nonstick skillet over medium heat, melt ½ tablespoon of the butter. Pour two ¼-cup portions of batter into the pan. When the edges of the pancakes begin to brown, turn them and cook on the other side for about 1 minute, or until browned. Transfer the pancakes to a serving plate and put it in the warm oven. Repeat to cook the remaining pancakes. Serve at once, topped with Onions Provençal.

Onions Provençal

Makes 2 cups

¼ cup olive oil

1 tablespoon minced garlic

3 to 4 red onions, thinly sliced

4 to 5 tomatoes, peeled, seeded, and cut into ½-inch dice (see page 134)

½ cup minced fresh basil

¼ cup minced fresh oregano

½ cup minced fresh parsley

Salt and freshly ground black pepper to taste

In a large, heavy skillet over high heat, heat the oil and cook the garlic until it is golden, about 1 minute.

Add the onions and reduce the heat to medium. Sauté for 6 to 8 minutes, or until the onions begin to brown.

Add the tomatoes, basil, oregano, and parsley, and cook for 4 to 6 minutes. Add the salt and pepper. Serve warm. Store in an airtight container in the refrigerator for up to 1 week.

Jalapeño-Cheese Corn Bread

Serves 8 to 10

Southwestern-style corn bread is not only a fine accompaniment to New World dishes, but it makes a great breakfast treat and a wonderful midnight snack.

2 cups cornmeal

1⅓ cups unbleached all-purpose flour

2½ tablespoons baking powder

⅓ teaspoon salt

¾ to 1 cup (3 to 4 ounces) shredded Monterey Jack cheese

3 eggs, beaten

¾ cup unpacked brown sugar

⅔ cup (1⅓ sticks) unsalted butter at room temperature

2 cups sour cream

2 tablespoons olive oil

2 cups fresh or frozen corn kernels (about 4 ears)

2 jalapeño chilies, seeded and minced

½ large red bell pepper, seeded, deveined, and finely diced

¼ cup honey

Preheat the oven to 350°F. In a medium bowl, combine the cornmeal, flour, baking powder, salt, and cheese.

In a large bowl, combine the eggs, then add the sugar and butter, then the sour cream, olive oil, corn kernels, jalapeños, and bell pepper.

Add the cornmeal mixture to the egg mixture and stir just until blended. Pour into a 9-by-13-inch baking dish and bake for 45 to 50 minutes, or until a toothpick inserted in the center comes out clean.

Remove from the oven and immediately drizzle the honey over the bread. Gently spread the honey over the corn bread with the back of a spoon, being careful not to damage the crust.

Spicy Cilantro-Corn Fritters

Makes 18 to 22 fritters

The foods that made the Americas great—corn and jalapeño chilies!

1 cup unbleached all-purpose flour

2 cups cornmeal

1 teaspoon salt

½ tablespoon baking powder

2 eggs

1 cup milk

¼ cup packed brown sugar

1 cup fresh or frozen corn kernels (about 2 ears)

½ cup finely chopped onion

2 jalapeño chilies, seeded and minced

1 teaspoon red pepper flakes

½ cup minced fresh cilantro

½ teaspoon ground cinnamon

4 to 6 cups vegetable oil

Preheat the oven to 250°F. In a large bowl, stir the flour, cornmeal, salt, and baking powder together.

In a medium bowl, whisk the eggs, milk, and brown sugar together. Gradually stir the wet mixture into the dry until blended. Stir in the corn kernels, onion, jalapeños, pepper flakes, cilantro, and cinnamon.

In a large, heavy pot or deep-fryer, heat the oil to 350°, or until fragrant. Using a 1½-inch ice cream scoop or measuring cup, drop five to seven ¼-inch scoops of batter into the hot oil and cook for 4 to 5 minutes, or until the fritters are golden brown. Using a slotted spoon, transfer to paper towels to drain. Put the fritters on a plate in the warm oven. Repeat with the remaining batter. Serve immediately.

Spanish Rice

Makes 4 cups

When Leon and I go out to different Cuban and Caribbean restaurants, we can judge the food just by tasting the rice and beans. For both of us, this food is our childhood recaptured.

Rice and beans are the "soul" of every meal at Cha Cha Cha. They're not as simple as they sound. With the beans, the key is the sofrito (page 34). With the rice, the key is the amount of water or chicken broth used. Like anything that matters to you, rice and beans need to be nourished, tended to, and most of all, loved.

⅓ cup olive oil

1 tablespoon minced garlic

½ red bell pepper, seeded, deveined, and cut into ¼-inch dice

1 green bell pepper, seeded, deveined, and cut into ¼-inch dice

2 bay leaves

1 onion, finely diced

½ tablespoon ground white pepper

1 tablespoon salt

¼ teaspoon ground turmeric

½ teaspoon bijol (optional)

5 cups chicken stock (page 14) or canned low-salt chicken broth

1 cup green Spanish olives, pitted

1 cup black olives, pitted

1 tomato, seeded and cut into ½-inch dice

1 bunch fresh cilantro, stemmed and minced

1 tablespoon capers, drained

2 cups white long-grain rice

In a heavy, medium saucepan over medium heat, heat the olive oil and cook the garlic, bell peppers, bay leaves, and onion until the onion is translucent, about 2 to 3 minutes.

Reduce the heat and add the white pepper, salt, turmeric, and optional *bijol*. Stir in the chicken stock or broth, olives, tomato, cilantro, and capers, then the rice. Bring to a boil, then cover and lower heat to a simmer. Cook for 20 minutes, or until the rice is tender. Fluff with a fork.

Cilantro Rice

Makes 6 to 8 cups   *This makes a great side dish, or a bed for Jerk Chicken (page 71).*

1 tablespoon unsalted butter or olive oil

1 carrot, peeled and finely diced

½ cup finely chopped scallions, including some green tops

2 cups white long-grain rice

½ teaspoon salt

½ cup minced fresh cilantro

4½ cups water

In a large, heavy saucepan, melt the butter or heat the olive oil over medium heat and sauté the carrot and scallions until the scallions soften, about 3 to 4 minutes.

Add the rice, salt, cilantro, and water. Stir and bring to a boil. Reduce the heat to low, cover, and cook the rice until tender, about 15 minutes. If the rice appears dry, add a touch more water. Let the rice stand uncovered for 3 to 5 minutes before serving.

Black Beans

Makes 6 to 8 cups

Every Cuban cook thinks his or her beans are the best, but I think my business partner's wife, Isabel Pak, makes the world's best beans. If only we could get her to spend more time in the kitchen and less time shopping, we would all be happier and, I'm sure, a good deal plumper.

1 pound (2 cups) dried black beans

8 cups water

1½ cups sofrito (page 34)

Salt and freshly ground black pepper to taste

Rinse and pick through the beans to remove any stones. In a large saucepan, combine the beans and water. Bring to a boil, then lower the heat and simmer for 1 hour, or until the beans are tender.

Add the sofrito and simmer for another 15 minutes. Add the salt and pepper. Drain and serve. Cover any leftover beans and store in the refrigerator.

Black Bean Cakes

Makes 8 cakes;
serves 4

Making black bean cakes is a little like making mud pies as a child. One of the keys to this recipe is how much or how little water is used in the cakes. With too much, the cake will slip and be difficult to handle; with too little, the cake will stick to your hands. Have fun, and remember, no throwing!

3 cups drained cooked black beans (page 61)

¼ cup minced fresh cilantro

2 scallions, finely chopped, including some green tops

½ red bell pepper, seeded, deveined, and cut into ¼-inch dice

½ teaspoon dried oregano

½ teaspoon ground cumin

1 tablespoon sesame seeds

1 tablespoon pumpkin seeds, toasted (see page 134)

3 tablespoons cornmeal

Salt and freshly ground black pepper to taste

2 cups Creole Sauce (page 46)

Preheat the oven to 350°F. Lightly oil an 8-inch square baking dish.

Place 1½ cups of the black beans in a blender or food processor and pulse for 30 seconds, or until the beans are coarsely pureed.

Pour the puree into a medium bowl and blend in the remaining 1½ cups beans and all the remaining ingredients except the salt, pepper, and sauce.

Pour into the prepared dish and bake, occasionally stirring, for 15 to 18 minutes, or until the beans begin to dry. Let cool to the touch. This makes the cakes easier to form. (Leave the oven on.)

Return the mixture to the same bowl and add salt and pepper. Wet your hands and form round bean cakes about 2½ inches in diameter and ½ inch thick. Place on a plate lined with waxed paper and refrigerate for at least 30 minutes. (The cakes are easier to cook when chilled.)

In a large nonstick skillet over medium heat, lightly brown the cakes on both sides, then place them on a baking sheet and bake for 3 to 5 minutes. Serve warm on a bed of the Creole sauce.

Savory Red Beans

Serves 6 to 8

Charles Reeves developed this recipe while visiting my cousin Gloria Pinette in Puerto Rico. Gloria's altars were the inspiration for the ones at Cha Cha Cha. She's a marvelous cook who has so far resisted all our efforts to lure her back to San Francisco.

These beans are great served with Pan-Seared New York Steak with Guava-Chipotle Ketchup (page 86), and also make a great soup when served with their own broth.

2 pounds (4 cups) dried red beans

1 gallon chicken stock (page 14), canned low-salt chicken broth, or water

5 tomatoes, seeded and chopped

10 garlic cloves, chopped

½ tablespoon ground white pepper

½ tablespoon ground cumin

3 dried New Mexico red chilies, seeded and left whole

2 cascabel chilies, seeded and left whole

3 pasilla chilies, seeded and cut into ⅛-inch-thick ribbons

3 canned jalapeño chilies, seeded and cut into ⅛-inch-thick ribbons

2 red bell peppers, seeded, deveined, and cut into ⅛-inch-thick ribbons

2 onions, cut into ⅛-inch-thick slices

½ teaspoon salt, or to taste

1 bunch fresh cilantro, stemmed and minced

Rinse the beans and pick through them for any stones. Soak the beans in hot water for 1 hour. Rinse the beans again. Place the beans in a stockpot with the stock, broth, or water, tomatoes, garlic, white pepper, cumin, and dried chilies. Bring to a boil, then reduce heat to a simmer and cook for 45 minutes.

Add the jalapeños, bell pepper, and onions. Cover and cook until the beans are tender, about 15 to 20 minutes. Add the salt and cilantro. These beans are best when reheated and served the next day.

Cinnamon-Scented Lentils

Makes 4 to 5 cups

3 cups dried lentils

¼ cup olive oil

½ red onion, finely diced

½ cup finely diced yellow onion

½ cup carrots, peeled and finely diced

½ cup finely diced celery

1 tablespoon minced garlic

1 red bell pepper, seeded, deveined, and finely diced

1 poblano chili, seeded and finely diced

6 cups water

¼ teaspoon ground cinnamon, or 1 cinnamon stick

Pinch of cayenne pepper

¼ teaspoon ground cumin

¼ teaspoon ground allspice

2 bay leaves

Salt and freshly ground black pepper to taste

Rinse and pick over the lentils for stones. Set aside.

In large, heavy saucepan over medium heat, heat the oil and sauté the onions until they are translucent, 3 to 4 minutes. Add the carrots, celery, garlic, bell pepper, and poblano. Continue to cook for 2 to 3 minutes, or until the vegetables are tender but firm.

Add the lentils, water, and remaining ingredients. Cook for 18 to 20 minutes, or until the lentils are tender but firm. Remove and discard the bay leaves and cinnamon stick, if using.

Chapter Four

Ochosi
POULTRY

Along with Ellegua and Oggún, Ochosi is one of the three primary warriors of Santería. He is the great hunter of the forest, tracking his prey with skill and speed, crossbow at the ready.

Ochosi is the *orisha* of prisons, for he symbolizes the freedom outside prison walls. Ochosi's judgment can be terrible and swift in punishing wrongdoers, but as do all the *orishas,* he delights in vindicating the innocent. There are many contemporary stories that tell of Ochosi's power to free those who have been falsely accused. A prayer and an offering to Ochosi is a strong remedy against one's enemies.

Ochosi is also the protector of all wildlife, especially wildfowl. It is his skill in hunting that has made him a favorite with Oloddumare and his followers. Ochosi's aim with bow and gun is so expert that his prey often shows no mark. Ochosi knows that hunting for one's food is a sacred privilege, to be respected. We are to be grateful for the bounty the world provides us.

Ochosi's colors are green, blue, and orange. His numbers are two and seven, and his days of worship are Monday and Tuesday. The Christian saint with whom he has been paired is St. Norbert. Ochosi has a weakness for anise, so his followers offer him foods made with aniseed, especially anise-flavored hardwater (liquor), to fortify his courage. His altars are commonly festooned with deer horns, arrows, and bullets. When Ochosi dances, he calls the animals to him with their own sounds and imitates their movements in the great forest.

Yucatán Chicken

Serves 6 to 8

Juan Morales, born and raised in Mexico City, created this recipe, which is based on the traditional Mayan dish cohinita pibil. *On the Yucatán peninsula, this dish is almost always made with pork; Juan has lightened it by using chicken.*

Juan's knowledge of chilies and other fiery ingredients has greatly enhanced our menu. Yucatán Chicken is not a nightly menu item, but is offered frequently as a special. The fragrances of banana leaf and achiote paste waft through the restaurant, and it's never long before the words "86 the Yucatán" are heard in the kitchen.

Juan says that the key to this recipe is keeping the fire low when grilling the chicken. This infuses the chicken with mesquite flavor.

Grated zest and juice of 1 lime

1 cup fresh orange juice

2 tablespoons fresh lemon juice

½ tablespoon dried oregano

3 canned chipotle chilies

½ cup achiote paste

½ tablespoon minced garlic

1 bay leaf

Salt and freshly ground pepper to taste

18 to 20 chicken legs, thighs, and breasts

Three 8-by-10-inch banana leaf pieces

1 cup chicken stock (see page 14) or canned low-salt chicken broth

Fresh cilantro sprigs

Lemon wedges

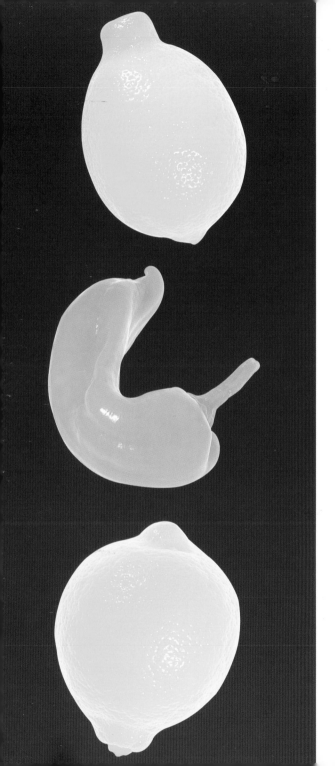

In a blender or food processor, combine the lime zest, citrus juices, oregano, chipotle chilies, achiote paste, garlic, and bay leaf and blend to a smooth puree. Add salt and pepper. Pour into a large bowl, add the chicken, cover, and refrigerate for at least 4 to 6 hours or overnight.

Light a fire in a charcoal or gas grill. Remove the chicken from the marinade at least 30 minutes before grilling, reserving the marinade. Preheat the oven to 350°F.

Put the chicken on the grill over a low fire, cover the grill, and cook the chicken, turning it frequently for 10 to 12 minutes, or until browned on both sides.

Lay a banana leaf piece in the bottom of an 8-inch square baking dish. Transfer the chicken to the baking dish. Pour the reserved marinade and the stock or broth over the chicken. Place a second banana leaf piece on top and cover the pan with aluminum foil. Bake for 15 to 18 minutes, or until the juices run clear when the meat is pierced with a knife.

Place the remaining banana leaf piece on a platter and place the cooked chicken on top. Spoon the cooking juices over and garnish with sprigs of fresh cilantro and lemon wedges. Serve immediately.

Jerk Chicken

Serves 6 to 8

Jerk chicken is one of Jamaica's national dishes. It might as well be called the national dish of Cha Cha Cha, it's so popular here. The enticement may be in the reggae music we often play, or it could be the habanero chili that dominates the flavor of the dish.

Jerk Chicken at Cha Cha Cha is a three-step process of marinating, baking and grilling. We serve it over our Cilantro Rice.

6 to 8 chicken legs and thighs

JERK MARINADE

1½ cups (12 ounces) dark beer

1 tablespoon olive oil

1 tablespoon minced garlic

4 bay leaves

¼ cup soy sauce

Grated zest of 1 lime

2 tablespoons fresh lime juice

1 bunch fresh cilantro, stemmed and minced

¼ to ½ teaspoon minced habanero chili

½ teaspoon ground allspice

½ teaspoon ground juniper berries

½ teaspoon salt

½ teaspoon ground white pepper

JERK SAUCE

½ cup tomato paste

¾ cup ½-inch-diced tomatoes

½ cup ½-inch-diced red bell peppers

½ cup ½-inch-diced green bell peppers

½ cup ½-inch-diced onions

2 tablespoons molasses

¾ cup golden raisins

2 cups chicken stock (page 14) or canned low-salt chicken broth

½ cup minced fresh cilantro

5 scallions, roughly chopped, including some green tops

½ teaspoon salt

Ground white pepper to taste

Cilantro Rice (page 60)

With a sharp knife, pierce 3 to 4 holes in each piece of chicken. In a large bowl, combine all the marinade ingredients. Add the chicken. Wearing rubber gloves, rub the marinade over each piece of chicken. Cover the bowl and refrigerate for at least 4 to 6 hours, or overnight.

Preheat the oven to 350°F. Place the sauce ingredients in a 12-by-20-inch roasting pan. Add the marinated chicken, mix, and cover tightly with aluminum foil.

Bake the chicken for 45 to 50 minutes, or until the juices run clear when the chicken is pierced with a knife. Meanwhile, light a fire in a charcoal or gas grill.

Transfer the chicken to the grill over a medium fire, using tongs. Grill on both sides for a total of 12 minutes. Meanwhile, puree the sauce in a blender or food processor. Taste and adjust the seasoning. Serve the chicken over Cilantro Rice and ladle the sauce over.

Chicken Mole Chalupa

Serves 6 to 8

Tamara Lutz, a native of Costa Rica, has been cooking at Cha Cha Cha for five years now. Tamara is a self-taught chef who honed her many skills in our kitchen. This recipe is a creative marriage of traditional Mexican cuisine and Tamara's Costa Rican heritage. The ingredients may seem endless, but once assembled, this exotic dish will dance on your palate.

This recipe calls for four different types of dried chilies, but fresh chilies may be substituted, or use one or two kinds of chilies, if you like.

One 3-pound chicken

1 teaspoon cumin seeds

1 teaspoon dried oregano

1 teaspoon sesame seeds, toasted (see page 134)

1 tablespoon tomato paste

½ cup water

1 tablespoon strong brewed coffee

1 tablespoon almonds, toasted and chopped (see page 132)

1 tablespoon peanut butter

1 square (1 ounce) 1 semisweet chocolate, finely chopped

1 teaspoon honey

½ teaspoon ground cinnamon

1 tablespoon minced fresh cilantro

1 teaspoon soy sauce

One-half 8-inch flour tortilla, toasted and crumbled (see page 134)

¼ cup vegetable oil

1 tablespoon coarsely chopped dried New Mexico red chili

1 tablespoon coarsely chopped dried chipotle chili

1 tablespoon coarsely chopped cascabel chili

1 tablespoon chopped pasilla chili

½ cup finely diced onion

½ tablespoon minced garlic

Place the chicken in a stockpot and add cold water to cover. Cover the pot, bring to a boil, reduce heat to a simmer and cook for 40 to 55 minutes, or until the chicken is tender and easily pulls away from the bone. Let cool to room temperature. Drain the chicken. Strain and reserve the broth. Remove and discard the skin, and pull the chicken off the bones in big pieces. Set aside.

In a large bowl, combine all the ingredients except the oil, chilies, onion, garlic, reserved broth, and chicken.

In a heavy, medium saucepan over medium heat, heat the oil and sauté the chilies, onion, and garlic for 3 to 5 minutes, or until the chilies begin to soften.

Lower the heat, add the ingredients in the large bowl, and cook for 3 to 5 minutes. Place the mixture in a blender or food processor and puree, adding some of the reserved broth if necessary to make a smooth sauce.

Return the sauce to the saucepan. Add the chicken and bring to a boil. Immediately remove from the heat and serve warm over rice and/or beans, in warm flour tortillas, or on a bed of salad greens.

Grilled Chicken Paillards with Dijon Mustard Sauce

Serves 4 to 6

Another of chef Jimmy Harris's signature dishes, and one of Cha Cha Cha's most popular. I can't say that there's much of a Caribbean influence in this recipe; I think we can attribute this unique dish to Jimmy's classical training.

This dish is very simple and fast to prepare—the hardest part may be getting the grill ready! The chicken breasts can even be cut and pounded the night before and refrigerated. Feel free to experiment with the sauce, using different mustards. This sauce would also be good with any grilled fish.

Eight 4-ounce skinless, boneless single chicken breasts

2 to 3 tablespoons olive oil

Dijon Mustard Sauce (following)

Cut each chicken breast lengthwise into 3 to 4 strips. Place the strips on a cutting board and, using the smooth side of a mallet, gently pound each piece to a ¼-inch thickness. Brush each piece with olive oil, cover, and refrigerate.

Light a charcoal or gas grill. Remove the chicken from the refrigerator 30 minutes before grilling.

Grill the chicken over a medium fire for 2 to 3 minutes on each side. Pool the mustard sauce on each plate and arrange 3 paillards on top. Serve at once.

Dijon Mustard Sauce

Makes 1½ cups

2 cups heavy cream

1 tablespoon Worcestershire sauce

2 to 3 tablespoons Dijon mustard

3 tablespoons minced fresh basil

¼ teaspoon salt

¼ teaspoon ground black pepper

In a medium saucepan, combine all the sauce ingredients. Place over medium heat and, stirring ocassionally, simmer for 15 to 20 minutes. Remove from heat and whisk for 1 or 2 minutes, or until the sauce begins to thicken. Taste and adjust the seasoning if necessary. Set aside and keep warm.

Grilled Quail with Southwestern Corn Bread Dressing and Roasted-Tomato Sauce

Serves 6

Andrew Gillen created the following dish. Born and raised in Glen Arbor, Michigan, Andrew credits his mom with being his first cooking instructor. After graduating from high school, Andrew moved to New Mexico, where he worked as a ski instructor to the Apache. In exchange, they taught him to cook with chilies and other native foods. Andrew has cooked for the Grateful Dead, various San Francisco neighborhood restaurants, and as a volunteer at community kitchens.

¼ cup olive oil

4 garlic cloves, crushed

1 tablespoon minced fresh oregano

1 tablespoon fresh lemon juice

1 tablespoon dry white wine

Pinch of cayenne pepper

12 semi-boneless quail

SOUTHWESTERN CORN BREAD DRESSING

1 recipe Jalapeño-Cheese Corn Bread (page 57)

2 tablespoons unsalted butter

1 cup fresh or frozen corn kernels (about 2 ears)

1 cup finely diced onions

1 tablespoon minced garlic

½ cup finely diced red bell pepper

½ cup finely diced poblano chili

2 eggs

2 cups (8 ounces) grated sharp Cheddar cheese

1½ tablespoons minced fresh oregano

½ teaspoon cayenne pepper

½ teaspoon salt

1 teaspoon ground black pepper

1½ cups chicken stock (page 14) or canned low-salt chicken broth

Roasted-Tomato Sauce (following)

In a large bowl, combine the oil, garlic, oregano, lemon juice, wine, and cayenne. Add the quail and coat the quail with the mixture. Cover and refrigerate for 4 to 6 hours or overnight.

To make the dressing: Preheat the oven to 350°F. Lightly oil a 9-by-13-inch baking dish. Crumble the corn bread into a large bowl. Set aside.

In a large, heavy skillet, melt the butter. Over high heat, sauté the corn and onions until golden, about 3 to 4 minutes.

Reduce heat to medium and add the garlic, bell pepper, and poblano. Sauté for 3 to 5 minutes, or until the pepper is tender but firm. Add to the corn bread.

In a medium bowl, combine the eggs, cheese, oregano, cayenne pepper, salt, and black pepper. Add this to the corn bread mixture and stir thoroughly. Add the chicken stock or broth and mix thoroughly again.

Put the dressing in the prepared dish and bake, stirring occasionally, for 50 to 55 minutes, or until the dressing is fluffy and still moist.

Light a fire in a charcoal or gas grill. Remove the quail from the refrigerator 30 minutes before cooking. Cook the quail over a medium fire, turning frequently, for 5 to 7 minutes, or until the skin is browned and the flesh is opaque throughout.

Serve with the corn bread dressing and Roasted-Tomato Sauce.

Roasted-Tomato Sauce

Makes 2 cups

6 fresh New Mexico red chilies

2 tablespoons olive oil

1 red onion, chopped

½ cup Cabernet Sauvignon wine

1½ cups chicken stock (page 14) or canned low-salt chicken broth

6 to 8 tomatoes, peeled and seeded (see page 134)

2 tablespoons minced garlic

1 teaspoon packed brown sugar

1 tablespoon minced fresh basil

1 teaspoon ground cumin

½ teaspoon dried thyme

½ teaspoon dried oregano

1 bay leaf

Salt to taste

Preheat the oven to 350°F. Place the chilies on a baking sheet and bake for 5 minutes, or until they are softened. Do not burn! Let the chilies cool to the touch. Remove and discard the skins and the seeds.

In a heavy, medium saucepan over medium heat, heat the olive oil and sauté the onion until it begins to brown, about 3 to 4 minutes.

Add the wine and stir to scrape up the browned bits from the bottom of the pan. Add the chicken stock or broth and cook to reduce by half.

Add the tomatoes, chilies, and all the remaining ingredients. Cook, stirring frequently, for 10 to 12 minutes, or until the sauce begins to thicken. Remove bay leaf. Puree in a blender or food processor. Serve warm.

Chapter Five

Oggún

MEATS

Oggún is the god of iron, of pure strength. He is also the god of war and of automobile and railroad accidents, so it is wise, as with all *orishas,* to respect his power and seek its proper balance.

The power of this Santería blacksmith and warrior is far-reaching and beyond compare. The proper balance of his power brings great fecundity to farms and ranches, ensuring food and strength for all. If the balance is wrong, however, war and chaos ensue. The weapons forged on Oggún's hearth may be used for aggression or for protection.

The followers of Oggún often display his symbols in their homes. Small iron cauldrons, no larger than six inches high, hold miniature versions of his *fundamentos,* the fundamental symbols through which he works. These replicas of rakes, hoes, machetes, and anvils must be kept sharp and cleaned with palm oil, in reverence of their great powers. Oggún's tools are brought forth from the earth, received in the rituals of warming blood and cooling herbs.

Oggún's colors are black and green; his numbers are three and seven; his days of worship are Monday and Tuesday. The saints he is identified with are Peter and Santiago. Offerings of alcohol and tobacco appease him and give him strength; his greatest appetite is for *agua diente,* the strongest of all Cuban liquors. Adorn his altar with iron weapons, tools, and other hardware. The dance of Oggún seems belligerent and threatening, as if marching to war, but it is only an expression of his natural forces.

Pan-Seared New York Steak with Guava-Chipotle Ketchup

Serves 6

This is another very successful dish at Cha Cha Cha. We have been asked over and over for the Guava-Chipotle Ketchup recipe, and perhaps one day we'll bottle it. The combination of beans and ketchup provide an instant barbecued flavor. Don't skimp on the steak! Serve with Savory Red Beans (page 63).

3 New York strip steaks, 10 ounces each

2 tablespoons ground cumin

Salt and freshly ground black pepper to taste

¼ cup olive oil

Guava-Chipotle Ketchup (following)

Cut the steaks in half lengthwise. Season with the cumin, salt, and pepper.

In a large cast-iron skillet over high heat, heat the olive oil until it begins to smoke. Sear the steaks for 3 to 4 minutes on each side for medium rare. Serve with Guava-Chipotle Ketchup.

Guava-Chipotle Ketchup

Makes 1½ cups

3 tablespoons guava paste

4 cups apple cider vinegar

1 cup packed brown sugar

1 tablespoon hoisin sauce

3 dried chipotle chilies,
stemmed and seeded

2 tablespoons Worcestershire
sauce

1 tablespoon molasses

2 tablespoons tomato paste

½ cup fresh orange juice

Combine all the ingredients in a heavy nonaluminum pot. Bring to a rolling boil, stirring occasionally. Reduce to a simmer and cook for 20 to 25 minutes, or until thick. Serve warm.

Marinated Cuban Steak with Tomatillo Salsa

Serves 6

Cuban steak is served two different ways at Cha Cha Cha: grilled and on sourdough bread at lunch, and over rice and beans at night. The marinade tenderizes the meat and gives it a unique sweet-and-sour flavor.

When selecting skirt steaks, ask your butcher for the outside cut, as the inside cut tends to be tough and chewy. This marinade also works well with top sirloin and rib-eye.

MARINADE

4 to 6 garlic cloves, minced

¼ bunch cilantro, stemmed and minced

¼ bunch parsley, stemmed and minced

2 tablespoons seasoned rice wine vinegar

1½ cups (12 ounces) dark beer

2 tablespoons fresh lemon juice

1 tablespoon minced fresh oregano

1 tablespoon soy sauce

Six 6- to 8-ounce skirt steaks, trimmed of fat

Tomatillo Salsa (following)

In a large bowl, combine all the marinade ingredients, then add the steaks, turning to coat them evenly. Cover and refrigerate for at least 2 to 4 hours, or overnight.

Light a fire in a charcoal or gas grill. Remove the meat from the refrigerator 30 minutes before grilling. Over a medium-hot fire, grill the steaks on both sides for a total of 6 minutes for medium rare. Serve with Tomatillo Salsa.

Tomatillo Salsa

Makes 2½ cups

2 pounds tomatillos, husked

¾ onion, coarsely chopped

6 garlic cloves

⅓ cup olive oil

2 jalapeño chilies, seeded

1 bunch fresh cilantro, stemmed

5 scallions, finely chopped, including some green tops

1 tablespoon red wine vinegar

¼ cup fresh lemon juice

⅓ cup tamarind juice

¼ cup molasses

Salt and freshly ground pepper to taste

1 red bell pepper, seeded, deveined, and cut into ¼-inch dice

3 tablespoons finely diced red onion

Preheat the oven to 375°F. Put the tomatillos, onion, and garlic in a baking pan. Drizzle the olive oil over and bake for 12 to 15 minutes, or until the tomatillos are slightly brown and soft.

Put the tomatillo mixture in a blender or food processor. Add the jalapeños, cilantro, scallions, vinegar, lemon juice, tamarind juice, and molasses, and puree.

Add salt and pepper. Stir in the red bell pepper and red onion.

Allspice-Crusted Lamb Chops with Roasted-Pepper Sauce

Serves 4

This dish, an engaging combination of Caribbean, California, and Southwestern influences, was created by Andrew Gillen. We use local lamb loin chops (Sonoma County lamb is the best in Northern California).

ALLSPICE CRUST

2 tablespoons whole allspice

2 tablespoons whole black pepper

1 tablespoon ground cumin

1 tablespoon packed brown sugar

1 tablespoon salt

Eight 1½-inch-thick lamb chops

¼ cup olive oil

Cinnamon-Scented Lentils (see page 64)

Roasted-Pepper Sauce (following)

Preheat the oven to 350°F. Put the allspice, pepper, cumin, and sugar in a spice grinder and grind to a fine powder. Mix in the salt.

Spread the allspice crust mixture in a shallow pan. Dip each chop into the mixture on both sides. Set aside.

In a large cast-iron skillet over medium heat, heat the olive oil and brown the lamb chops on both sides, about 8 minutes total. Be careful not to burn the crust.

Place the chops on a baking sheet lined with aluminum foil and bake for 6 to 8 minutes for medium rare. Serve with the Roasted-Pepper Sauce and Cinnamon-Scented Lentils.

Roasted-Pepper Sauce

Makes 1½ cups

3 red bell peppers

½ tablespoon unsalted butter

2 shallots, diced

4 garlic cloves, crushed

½ onion, finely chopped

½ carrot, peeled and finely chopped

½ cup dry white wine

1½ cups chicken stock (page 14) or canned low-salt chicken broth

2 cups heavy cream

¼ teaspoon red pepper flakes

Salt and freshly ground pepper to taste

Preheat the broiler. Char the peppers until blackened all over. Place them in a paper bag and seal it. When the peppers are cool to the touch, after about 15 minutes, peel off the skin. Seed, dice, and set the peppers aside.

In a medium, heavy saucepan, melt the butter over medium heat and sauté the shallots, garlic, onions, and carrot for 3 to 5 minutes, or until tender but still firm.

Add the wine and stir to scrape the browned bits from the bottom of the pan. Cook to reduce by half. Add the chicken stock or broth and cook to reduce by half.

Add the cream, peppers, and pepper flakes. Bring to a slow boil, reduce the heat to a simmer, and cook, whisking occasionally, for 12 to 15 minutes, or until the sauce thickens.

Puree the sauce in a blender or food processor. Add salt and pepper. Serve warm.

Grilled Pork Chops with Mango Chutney

Serves 4 to 6

This wonderful recipe turns ordinary pork chops into a Caribbean fiesta. The marinade infuses the flavors of the spices, salt, sugar, and herbs into the chops. Years ago, before refrigeration, this kind of marinade also served to preserve foods and tenderize game. You will need to prepare the marinade one day ahead.

BRINE MARINADE

8 cups water

½ cup salt

¼ cup packed brown sugar

4 whole allspice

3 juniper berries, crushed

8 black peppercorns

3 bay leaves

½ bunch fresh thyme

5 garlic cloves, smashed

3 whole cloves

1 teaspoon minced fresh ginger

Eight 5- to 6-ounce pork chops
Roasted-Garlic Sweet Potatoes (page 51)
Mango Chutney (page 47)

Place all the marinade ingredients in a large nonaluminum stockpot and bring to a boil. Cook for 5 to 7 minutes. Remove from heat and let cool overnight.

Submerge the pork chops in the marinade for 45 minutes. Light a fire in a charcoal or a gas grill. Grill the pork chops on both sides over a medium-hot fire for 8 to 10 minutes, or until the pork chops are firm and cooked through. Serve with Roasted-Garlic Sweet Potatoes and Mango Chutney.

Chapter Six

Yemayá

FISH AND SHELLFISH

When men and women meet, when they join in creating, when they are united, they inhabit the realm of Yemayá, for she is birth and existence, the essence of the life-sustaining fluids of the body and of the world. Yemayá is the giver of life. She is the tide of the oceans, the flow of the rivers, the swaying hips in a rhythmic *danzon.*

Yemayá is the goddess of motherhood, the *orisha* charged with the protection of children. Kind and forgiving, she is the embodiment of the great maternal life force we all need to guide us. It takes a great offense to turn Yemayá against one of her children. She is as full and encompassing as the oceans themselves.

In her beneficence, she has given her children two great and precious gifts. We owe to Yemayá the creation of the seashells, sacred objects the *orishas* use to communicate with their followers, and through which their wisdom is passed on to mortals. It is also through Yemayá that the beauty of the rainbow came to the world. Oloddumare presented the rainbow to Yemayá as her crown, in thanks for all the sons and daughters she had created.

Yemayá rides her oceans in a majestic silver boat, and she is adorned there with the treasures of her sea, in a turquoise tunic that gleams with the scales of a thousand fish, her black hair netted with pearls and shells. During storms, she appears as a mermaid who will save those in peril. And when she appears on land, her beauty is so awesome that all who see her fall into a rapturous silence.

Yemayá is the richest of all of the *orishas* because she rules over not only the ocean's natural bounties, but also those treasures that fall into the ocean in storm and shipwreck. She is the patron of sailors and mariners, stevedores and bargemen, and all who travel on the seas.

Yemayá's colors are blue and white; her number is seven; her day of worship is Saturday. She has been syncretized with St. Regla. Offerings to Yemayá include flowers, fruits, *chicharrones,* and fried bananas. Her altar is decorated with fans, seashells, pearls, and fishing nets. Her dance is like that of the ocean itself, sometimes calm and soothing, sometimes tempestuous.

Spicy Fried Calamari

Serves 6

Nearby Monterey Bay is where great quantities of squid are caught, and 1801 Haight Street is where great quantities are consumed. You must make this recipe, and it has to be served with Lemon Aioli (page 40). Remember, if you're afraid of this dish for any reason, bring your copy of the book into the restaurant, and we'll give you a plate on the house.

5 tablespoons all-purpose flour

5 tablespoons Cajun Spice Mix (see page 35)

9 to 12 squid, 5 to 7 inches long, cleaned and sliced (see page 134)

3 to 4 cups canola oil

Lemon or lime wedges

1 cup Lemon Aioli (page 40)

Place the flour and Cajun spice mix in a large bowl and mix. Add the squid and turn until all the pieces are thoroughly coated. Shake off the excess mixture.

In a large, heavy pot or deep-fryer over medium heat, heat the oil to 375°F, or until almost smoking.

Fry the squid for 2 to 3 minutes, or until a light golden brown. Using a slotted spoon, transfer to paper towels to drain. Serve immediately with lemon or lime wedges and Lemon Aioli.

Snapper in Banana Leaves

Serves 8

Banana leaves have been used for centuries in Amerindian cooking. Here, they are folded into packets for baking fish fillets, which keeps the fish juicy and infuses it with an exotic smoky scent. The spice paste gives the fish a great color, and the banana salsa, created by our own Gabriela Salas, a native of Costa Rica, adds a New World flavor to this criollo *cousin of fish* en papillote. *This marinade and cooking method also work well with boneless chicken.*

SPICE PASTE

¼ cup fresh lime juice

¼ cup annatto oil (see page 132)

½ cup minced fresh cilantro

1 tablespoon finely chopped scallion, white part only

1 tablespoon minced garlic

2 tablespoons Worcestershire sauce

1 teaspoon salt

1 teaspoon ground black pepper

2 teaspoons red wine vinegar

Eight 8-ounce red snapper fillets

Eight banana leaves (optional)

Eight ¼-inch-thick lime slices

Gabriela's Banana Salsa (page 39)

To make the spice paste: Place all the ingredients in a blender or food processor and blend to a smooth paste. Place the fish in a large bowl and pour the spice paste over it; coat the fish evenly. Cover and marinate in the refrigerator for 1 to 2 hours.

Preheat the oven to 350°F. Cut eight 8-by-10-inch pieces of banana leaf or aluminum foil. Place 1 marinated fish fillet in the center of each piece of leaf or foil. Coat the fish well with the spice paste and top with 1 slice of lime. Fold the leaf or foil over the fish to make a package that completely encloses the fish.

Place on a baking sheet and bake for 8 to 10 minutes, or until the fish is opaque throughout.

Serve the fish in its leaf wrapping. If you used foil, unwrap the fish and remove the foil. Serve at once with the banana salsa.

Salmon Croquettes with Tomato Coulis

Makes 12
croquettes

Honduran native José Rodriquez, who created this dish, is one of the most creative innovators of fish and shellfish I've ever met. This salmon recipe is his masterpiece. It works well for a main dish, or as an appetizer.

1 pound salmon fillet

2 tablespoons Cajun Spice Mix (page 35)

1 teaspoon salt

¼ cup finely chopped onion

2 tablespoons finely chopped poblano chili

2 tablespoons finely chopped red bell pepper

2 tablespoons finely chopped celery

½ teaspoon minced garlic

2½ tablespoons flour

½ cup dried bread crumbs

4 cups canola oil for frying

Tomato Coulis (following)

Preheat the oven to 400°F. Sprinkle the salmon fillet with the Cajun Spice Mix and ½ teaspoon of the salt.

Place the salmon in a lightly oiled baking dish and bake for about 5 to 7 minutes (depending on the thickness of the fillet), or until the salmon is firm to the touch and slightly translucent in the center.

With a slotted spatula, remove the fish, drain on paper towels, and let cool to room temperature.

Place the salmon in a large bowl and gently crumble the fish. Add the remaining ½ teaspoon salt and all the remaining ingredients except the bread crumbs, canola oil, and tomato coulis.

With your hands, blend the mixture together evenly and form into 3-by-1-inch cylinders, or croquettes. Roll each croquette in the bread crumbs and place on a baking sheet lined with waxed paper. Refrigerate for 1 hour.

In a large, heavy pot or deep-fryer, heat the oil to 325° to 350°F, or until fragrant, and fry the croquettes for 2 to 4 minutes, or until golden brown. Drain on paper towels; serve immediately with Tomato Coulis.

Tomato Coulis

Makes 2 cups

4 to 5 tomatoes, peeled and seeded (see page 134)

¼ bunch fresh basil, stemmed and julienned

2 tablespoons extra-virgin olive oil

Salt and freshly ground black pepper to taste

Puree the tomatoes in a blender or food processor. Pour into a fine-meshed sieve lined with cheesecloth and place over a bowl. Let drain for 2 to 4 hours.

Pour the tomato puree into a medium bowl and stir in the remaining ingredients. Serve immediately.

Blackened Pacific Salmon Quesadillas with Chipotle Cream

Serves 4

According to culinary legend, blackening was created by the Cajuns of the Louisiana Delta as a way to liven up the taste of poor-quality meats and fish. When the best cuts and fillets are used, the results are even better, of course.

One 12-ounce salmon fillet, 1 to 2 inches thick, cut into 4 pieces

1 cup Blackening Spices (page 37)

4 tablespoons vegetable oil

¼ cup finely diced yellow onion

¼ cup finely diced tomato

¼ cup finely diced green bell pepper

⅓ cup finely diced eggplant

1 teaspoon minced garlic

2 tablespoons minced fresh cilantro

Four to five 10-inch flour tortillas

1 cup (4 ounces) shredded Monterey Jack cheese

Chipotle Cream (following) or Spicy Guacamole (page 24)

Preheat the oven to 325°F. Line a baking sheet with aluminum foil. Dredge the salmon fillets in the blackening spices. Set aside.

Place a medium cast-iron skillet over high heat. When the pan begins to smoke, in 3 to 5 minutes, add 2 tablespoons of the oil and immediately put the salmon in the pan. Cook for 2 to 3 minutes, or until the blackening spices crust. Turn the heat down and carefully turn the salmon fillet over. Cook for 2 to 3 minutes, or until the blackening spices crust. Drain on paper towels.

Wipe the skillet clean and place over high heat. Add the remaining 2 tablespoons oil and sauté the vegetables, garlic, and cilantro for 3 to 4 minutes, or until the vegetables are tender. Reduce the heat and gently flake the salmon into the vegetables, then remove the mixture from heat and set aside.

On a clean work surface, lay out the tortillas and sprinkle the cheese evenly on them, leaving a ½-inch space around the edge. Place the salmon mixture on one side of the tortilla and fold the tortilla in half. Place the quesadillas in the prepared pan. Lightly brush the quesadillas with oil and bake for 3 to 5 minutes. Remove from the oven and, with a pizza cutter or very sharp knife, cut each quesadilla into 3 portions. Serve with Chipotle Cream or guacamole.

Chipotle Cream

Makes ¾ cup

½ **cup heavy cream**

Grated zest of 1 lemon

Juice of 2 lemons

½ **teaspoon minced fresh thyme**

1 tablespoon sour cream

1 tablespoon minced canned chipotle

½ **teaspoon minced shallot**

Pour the cream in a medium bowl. Add all the remaining ingredients and whisk together until the cream begins to froth a little.

Skillet Cajun Shrimp

Serves 4 to 5

This is by far our most popular dish, and another of chef Jimmy Harris's inspired creations. We serve it in individual cast-iron skillets (you can use a shallow bowl) to allow plenty of room for soaking up the spice-infused cream sauce.

½ cup Cajun Spice Mix
(page 35)

1½ cups (12 ounces) dark beer

2 cups heavy cream

1 pound medium shrimp, peeled and deveined (see page 134)

½ teaspoon red pepper flakes

In a large, heavy saucepan, mix the Cajun spice mix and beer. Cook over medium heat, stirring constantly with a wire whisk to make a thick paste. Do not allow the the mixture to burn.

Gradually stir in the cream to make a smooth sauce. Cook over medium heat, stirring occasionally, for 8 to 10 minutes, or until the sauce thickens slightly and turns a rich rust color.

Add the shrimp and red pepper flakes. Reduce the heat and cook shrimp over low heat for 2 to 3 minutes, or until the shrimp are pink and opaque.

Taste and adjust the seasoning. Serve in individual skillets or bowls with your favorite bread.

Rock Shrimp Run Down

Serves 4 to 6

"Run down" is a Caribbean term for cooking up all the leftovers in your refrigerator with coconut milk. Christine Oncken, who has cooked at Cha Cha Cha for many years, was inspired to create this run down recipe after traveling in the Caribbean. It's a versatile dish that goes great with salmon, lobster, or crab. It can also be prepared with vegetables only.

1 russet baking potato

½ teaspoon unsalted butter

2 shallots, minced

1 red bell pepper, seeded, deveined, and cut into ¼-inch dice

1 teaspoon minced garlic

¼ teaspoon minced fresh ginger

1¾ cups (14 ounces) coconut milk

½ jalapeño chili, seeded and minced

4 scallions, finely chopped, including some green tops

2 tomatoes, seeded and cut into ¼-inch dice

1 pound rock shrimp, peeled and deveined (see page 134)

1 teaspoon minced fresh thyme

2 tablespoons fresh lime juice

Salt and freshly ground black pepper to taste

4 to 6 fresh cilantro sprigs

Grated lime zest to taste

Cut the potato into ¼-inch dice and cook in salted boiling water for 2 to 3 minutes. Drain and set aside. In an large, heavy saucepan, melt the butter and sauté the shallots, bell pepper, garlic, and ginger for 1 to 2 minutes, or until the shallots are translucent. Add the coconut milk and reduce the heat to medium.

Add the jalapeño, scallions, tomatoes, and potato. Add the rock shrimp and cook, stirring, for 3 to 5 minutes, or until the shrimp are pink and opaque. Add the thyme, lime juice, salt, and pepper.

Serve in shallow bowls, garnished with a cilantro sprig and lime zest.

Steamed New Zealand Mussels

Serves 2

At Cha Cha Cha we use New Zealand mussels for their beautiful shells, uniform size, and intense, sweet flavor. Black mussels from North America will lend a more tangy flavor.

4 to 5 tablespoons olive oil

12 mussels, scrubbed and debearded

1 teaspoon minced garlic

1 tomato, peeled, seeded, and cut into ¼-inch dice (see page 134)

2 scallions, finely chopped, including some green tops

1 tablespoon minced fresh cilantro

⅛ teaspoon minced habanero chili, or 1/4 teaspoon red pepper flakes

½ cup Chardonnay wine

¼ teaspoon sea salt

½ cup fish stock (page 13) or clam juice

4 to 5 saffron threads

1 lemon or lime, cut into wedges

2 fresh cilantro sprigs

In a large, heavy pot over medium heat, heat the olive oil and sauté the mussels, garlic, tomato, scallions, cilantro, and habanero chili or red pepper flakes for 3 to 5 minutes, or until garlic is translucent. Do not allow the bottom of the pan or any ingredients to brown.

Add the wine, salt, fish stock, and saffron. Cover, increase the heat slightly, and cook for 3 to 4 minutes, or until the mussels open. Discard any mussels that do not open.

Divide the mussels among 2 shallow bowls and pour the cooking juices over them. Serve with lemon or lime wedges and a cilantro sprig.

Buttermilk Fried Oysters

Serves 2

Charles Reeves, who created this recipe, stresses that you should serve oysters only during months that have the letter "R" in them. Always buy your oysters from a reputable seafood dealer, and inquire about their origins. Only the freshest will do.

3 eggs

2 cups buttermilk

12 oysters, shucked

1 cup all-purpose flour

1 cup fine cornmeal

¼ cup olive oil

¾ cup Island Barbecue Sauce (page 45)

In a large bowl, beat the eggs and mix in the buttermilk.

Dredge each oyster in the flour, then in the buttermilk mixture, and lastly in the cornmeal. Put on waxed paper.

In a large cast-iron skillet over medium heat, heat the oil until almost smoking. Carefully place the oysters in the pan.

Fry on each side for 1 to 2 minutes, or until golden brown. Drain on paper towels. Serve with Island Barbecue Sauce.

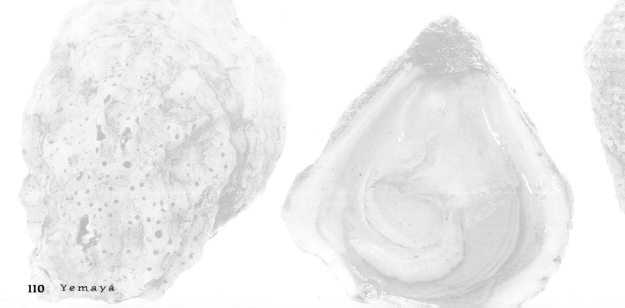

Sautéed Sea Scallops with Chipotle-Orange Sauce

Serves 4

Chef Patty Stirling decided that she wanted her cooking to be "bright," as exemplified by this dish, which is bright in taste, temperature, and color. She thought that the atmosphere at Cha Cha Cha was bright, and when she was working, I always played cassettes of the Cuban bandleader Machito to keep it that way.

2 tablespoons unsalted butter

1 pound sea scallops

1 tablespoon minced garlic

1 tablespoon minced shallots

3 to 4 canned chipotle chilies, finely chopped

¼ cup dry white wine

Juice of 3 oranges

1½ cups heavy cream

Grated zest of 1 orange

2 tablespoons minced fresh cilantro

½ recipe Cilantro Rice (page 60)

In a large, heavy skillet, melt 1½ tablespoons of the butter over high heat. When the butter begins to brown, add the scallops and reduce the heat to medium. Sauté the scallops for 3 to 4 minutes, turning to brown them on both sides. Drain on paper towels. Pour off the butter and wipe the pan clean with paper towels.

In the same pan, melt the remaining ½ tablespoon butter. Over medium heat sauté the garlic, shallots, and chipotle chilies for 1 to 2 minutes, or until the garlic is translucent.

Add the wine, stir, and cook to reduce by half. Add the orange juice and cook to reduce by two thirds. Add the cream, zest, and cilantro. Reduce the heat to low and, stirring often, cook for 8 to 10 minutes, or until the sauce thickens.

Reheat the scallops in the sauce for 2 to 3 minutes. Serve immediately over Cilantro Rice.

Ceviche

Serves 4 to 5

This great dinner party dish can be made the night before. The lemon and lime juice do most of the cooking. Our recipe calls for scallops, shrimp, and salmon, but other fish and shellfish that work well are octopus, lobster, and tuna. When making ceviche, use only the freshest available fish and shellfish.

The Scotch bonnet chili used in this dish is the hottest of the chilies. Wear rubber gloves when handling it, and wash your hands in hot soapy water when finished. Lizano is a Costa Rican marinade with a turmeric base.

6 ounces bay scallops

2 to 3 ounces salmon or snapper fillet, cut into ¼-inch dice

½ cup fresh lemon juice

¼ cup sparkling water

Pinch of sugar

4 ounces jumbo shrimp, peeled and deveined (see page 134)

1 tablespoon minced fresh cilantro

⅛ teaspoon Scotch bonnet chili, minced, or ¼ teaspoon red pepper flakes

2 tablespoons finely chopped red onion

2 tablespoons finely chopped red bell pepper

2 tablespoons *lizano* (optional)

½ teaspoon minced garlic

Grated zest and juice of 1 lime

Salt and freshly ground black pepper to taste

Mixed baby greens

Place the scallops and salmon or snapper in a medium bowl with the lemon juice, sparkling water, and sugar. Cover and refrigerate for 3 to 4 hours.

Blanch the shrimp in salted boiling water for 1 to 2 minutes. Drain and plunge them into ice water, then drain on paper towels. Cut each shrimp in half lengthwise.

Put the shrimp in the marinade with the scallops. Gently stir in the cilantro, chili or pepper flakes, onion, bell pepper, *lizano*, garlic, lime zest and juice, salt, and pepper.

Cover and refrigerate overnight. Drain, reserving the juice, and serve on a bed of mixed baby greens in shallow bowls, ladling 2 to 4 tablespoons of the juice over each serving.

Bill's Zarzuela

Serves 6 to 8

This recipe was created by Bill Higgins, executive chef at Cha Cha Cha. A chef since the age of seventeen, his eclectic experience includes classical French, "Floribbean," New American, Japanese, and the New World cuisine that has become popular at Cha Cha Cha.

Bill knows that the key to a great zarzuela, or any seafood dish, is to not over-cook the seafood. He always makes sure his guests are sitting down and ready to eat before he adds the shrimp, scallops, and squid. This ensures that the fish will be perfectly cooked and still hot.

¼ cup olive oil

1 onion, finely chopped

1 red bell pepper, seeded, deveined, and thinly sliced

1 green bell pepper, seeded, deveined, and thinly sliced

1 fresh fennel bulb, thinly sliced

1½ tablespoons tomato paste

10 garlic cloves, minced

1½ pounds tomatoes, peeled, seeded, and chopped (see page 134)

5 scallions, green tops removed, finely chopped

2 bay leaves

¼ cup fresh lemon juice

6 saffron threads

½ cup dry white wine or brandy

2 cups fish stock (page 13) or clam juice

1 tablespoon minced canned chipotle chili, or 1 teaspoon red pepper flakes

Salt and freshly ground pepper to taste

12 clams, scrubbed

12 mussels, scrubbed and debearded

⅓ cup each finely chopped fresh basil, oregano, and Italian parsley

12 medium shrimp

12 bay scallops

¾ pound squid, cleaned and sliced (see page 134)

Lemon and lime wedges

In a large, heavy pot over high heat, heat the olive oil and sauté the onion, peppers, fennel, tomato paste, and garlic for 3 to 5 minutes, or until the onions are translucent.

Add the tomatoes, scallions, bay leaves, lemon juice, saffron, white wine, fish stock or clam juice, chipotle chili or pepper flakes, salt, and pepper. Reduce the heat and simmer for 7 to 10 minutes, stirring often.

Add the clams, mussels, and herbs, cover, and reduce the heat slightly. Cook for 6 to 8 minutes, or until the clams and mussels open. Discard any clams or mussels that do not open.

Add the shrimp, scallops, and squid, and cook for 4 to 6 minutes, or until the shrimp are pink and opaque. Taste and adjust the seasoning. Garnish with lemon and lime wedges. Serve immediately with Spanish Rice.

Gumbo Doucet

Serves 10 to 12

Originating in New Orleans, gumbo evolved from the influences of Cajun, French, Acadian, African, and Spanish cuisines. This gumbo recipe brings the taste buds alive with a heat that increases with each bite.

There are many steps in the preparation of a gumbo, including the making of the stock, the roux, the rice, and cooking the crab. David Doucet (Louisiana born and raised) created this recipe. While living in San Francisco, David became homesick for a pot of his mother's gumbo, and after numerous calls home and more than a few good gumbo parties, here it is. Or as they say in N'Orleans, "D'ere 'tis!"

Oh, yes, one more detail. The gumbo always turns out better if you listen to New Orleans music during the cooking. David prefers Professor "Long Hair" Kelter, also known as Fess.

BROWN ROUX

2 cups vegetable oil

2 cups all-purpose flour

2 cups finely chopped onions

1 cup finely chopped celery

1 cup finely chopped green bell pepper

2 tablespoons minced garlic

1½ tablespoons ground black pepper

1½ tablespoons ground white pepper

1½ tablespoons cayenne pepper

1 tablespoon dried thyme

1 tablespoon dried oregano

12 cups fish stock (page 13) or clam juice

4 live Dungeness crabs

1½ pounds andouille sausage

Salt and freshly ground black pepper to taste

1 tablespoon minced fresh parsley

30 oysters, shucked

20 medium shrimp, peeled

¼ teaspoon filé, or 1 tablespoon crab boil

Steamed white rice for serving

To make the roux: In a large, heavy pot over medium heat, heat the oil and gradually stir in the flour. Continue cooking, stirring constantly and adjusting the heat as necessary to prevent burning, until the roux has turned brown, 15 to 20 minutes. Add all the remaining ingredients and cook, stirring constantly, for 5 to 7 minutes. Be careful of the steam that rises from this process. Set aside and cool to room temperature. Use at once, or cover and refrigerate for up to 1 week.

In a stockpot, bring the fish stock or clam juice to a boil. Place one of the crabs on a work surface with the rear of the crab toward you. Using both hands, grasp the legs and claw on each side of the body. Strike the underside of the shell a sharp blow against the edge of a table; this stuns the crab. Put the crab into the stock or juice and cook for 5 to 7 minutes. Remove the crab. Repeat with the remaining crabs. Let the crabs cool to the touch. Reduce the stock to a simmer.

Pull off the top shell and the triangular breastplate on the bottom of each crab. Remove and discard the white gills above the legs, the firm white crooked intestine in the middle of the back, and the mouth parts. Pour the crab butter out of the body. Break the legs off the crab and crack the legs and claws lightly with a hammer or mallet. Cut the body lengthwise and crosswise into 4 pieces with a cleaver or large knife. Set aside.

Bring the stock to a slow boil over medium heat. Stir in the roux a little at a time until the gumbo is thick and rich. Cook for 10 to 12 minutes, stirring occasionally.

Meanwhile, grill or pan-fry the andouille sausage until it is evenly browned. Cut into ½-inch slices. Add to the gumbo. Add the salt, pepper, and parsley.

Just before serving, add the oysters, shrimp, crab (both body and legs), and filé or crab boil. Cook for 5 to 7 minutes, or until the shrimp are pink and firm. Serve over steamed white rice.

Chapter Seven

Oshún

DESSERTS AND DRINKS

The last of the goddesses to be created, Oshún is the oracle of Santería, who can predict the future and clarify the past. She is also the messenger Oloddumare sends when he wishes to speak with his *orishas*.

Oshún's powers in this world are great. She is the goddess of marriage and fertility, as well as the goddess of money and gold. Sacrifices to Oshún help to establish one's family and to ensure its well-being.

The natural force with which Oshún is entrusted is that of the rivers, or as many Santeros say in English, the "sweetwaters." The purity and clarity of the sweetwaters, on which all life depends, we owe to her.

It is often said of Oshún's beauty and her character that it is like honey, sweet and delicious, but potent, almost a little too powerful. A bit of her refinements, like dessert, is a necessary joy that lasts a long, long time. She can be coy and seductive, but one must be wary of her power. Like all the orishas, she demands a balanced respect. The goddess of charity, she can be generous to her believers.

Oshún's colors are yellow, gold, and white; her number is five. Appropriately, her day of worship is Saturday, a wedding day. Her Catholic counterpart is St. Caridad. The offerings that please her most are elaborately decorated candies, honey in all forms, and sunflowers. Decorate her altar with fans, gold coins (especially chocolate-filled ones), and peacock feathers. When she dances, she plays the part of the coquette, simultaneously seductive and distant.

Plantain-Peanut Bread

Serves 8 to 10

This sweet bread makes a wonderful dessert, and is also great toasted for breakfast, with your favorite jam.

8 eggs

1½ cups packed brown sugar

1 cup (2 sticks) unsalted butter at room temperature

3 cups unbleached all-purpose flour

½ tablespoon baking powder

1 teaspoon salt

6 ripe plantains

1½ cups (9 ounces) unsalted peanuts

Preheat the oven to 350°F. In a large bowl, whisk the eggs until well blended. Gradually whisk in the brown sugar, then gradually blend in the butter.

Stir the flour, baking powder, and salt together and stir it into the mixture until smooth.

Puree 4 of the plantains. Cut the remaining 2 plantains into ¼-inch dice. Gently stir the puree, the diced plantains, and the peanuts into the mixture.

Pour into a buttered 9-by-13-inch baking pan. Bake for 45 to 50 minutes, or until a toothpick inserted in the center of the bread comes out clean. Let cool and cut into squares to serve.

Pineapple-Plantain Coconut Bread with Raisin Sauce

Serves 8 to 12

. . . he takes the pass in full stride, jukes, turns, shoots. Another score at the buzzer, and Pete Hood brings home another victory . . . *I just know that's what's going on in his head as he orchestrates the ballet of another hectic brunch, turning, pointing, cajoling, ordering, totally in his element, on the court or behind the stove. There's Pete, sending out tasty and beautiful plates from the controlled chaos of the Cha Cha Cha kitchen.*

Here's one of Pete's best creations. This sweet bread is great served warm or cold, for breakfast, lunch, or dinner. Feel free to substitute any combination of fruits and nuts you like: bananas, papaya, dates, raisins, walnuts, almonds, whatever. For dessert, serve warm with vanilla ice cream.

3 cups unbleached all-purpose flour

1 tablespoon baking powder

1½ teaspoons baking soda

1½ teaspoons salt

1 teaspoon ground cinnamon

½ teaspoon ground nutmeg

3 eggs, beaten

½ cup milk

1 cup coconut milk

4 tablespoons butter, melted

¾ cup sugar

1 teaspoon vanilla extract

2 to 3 ripe plantains, cut into ¼-inch dice

1½ cups ½-inch-diced pineapple

¼ cup pecans, chopped

¼ cup dried coconut flakes

Raisin Sauce (following)

Preheat the oven to 350°F. Lightly oil and flour two 9-by-5-inch loaf pans. In a medium bowl, combine the flour, baking powder, baking soda, salt, cinnamon, and nutmeg. In a large bowl, combine the eggs, milk, coconut milk, melted butter, sugar, and vanilla.

Stir the wet ingredients into the dry ingredients, then blend in the plantains, pineapple, pecans, and coconut flakes.

Pour the batter into the prepared pans and bake for 55 to 60 minutes, or until a toothpick inserted in the center of the bread comes out clean. Allow to cool slightly before serving with the raisin sauce.

Raisin Sauce

Makes 1½ cups

1¾ cups (14 ounces) coconut milk

3 tablespoons Kahlúa

¼ cup dark raisins

¼ cup dried coconut flakes

1 tablespoon unsalted butter

In a small saucepan, bring 1 cup of the coconut milk and the Kahlúa to a low boil over medium heat. Add the raisins and cook for 1 to 2 minutes, or until they are soft. Pour the mixture into a blender or food processor and puree until smooth. Return to the pan and add the coconut flakes and the remaining ¾ cup coconut milk. Bring to a boil for 30 seconds, then remove from heat and stir in the butter. Serve warm.

Coconut-Vanilla Flans

Serves 4

This popular Cuban dessert can be made 2 days in advance of your next dinner party. This flan is not only famous in Cuba but also in San Francisco's Haight Ashbury, where at Cha Cha Cha our pastry chef can't keep up with the demand. When making the flan, take extra care in caramelizing the sugar. Over-caramelizing will make the flan taste burnt.

¾ cup sugar

2 tablespoons water

1 cup evaporated milk

⅔ cup sweetened condensed milk

½ cup coconut milk

4 eggs

2 egg yolks

1 tablespoon vanilla extract

½ teaspoon salt

¼ cup dried coconut flakes, toasted (see page 132)

Preheat the oven to 350°F. In a heavy, medium saucepan, combine ½ cup of the sugar with the water. Boil over high heat until the sugar has turned an amber color, about 5 minutes. Divide the caramelized sugar evenly among 6-ounce custard cups. Set aside.

In a medium saucepan, combine the milks and the remaining ¼ cup sugar. Cook over high heat until bubbles form around the sides of the pan.

In a large bowl, whisk the eggs, egg yolks, vanilla, and salt together. Gradually whisk the scalded milk into the egg mixture, without scrambling the eggs. Strain and pour into the custard cups.

Place the cups in a baking dish and fill the baking dish half full with hot water. Sprinkle the coconut on the flans. Cover the baking dish with aluminum foil and bake for 40 to 45 minutes, or until a knife inserted in the center of a flan comes out clean. Let cool in the baking dish.

To serve, run a knife around the inside edge of each custard cup and turn upside down onto a dessert plate.

Sangría Cha Cha Cha

Makes 8 cups

Salvado Rodriguez prepares our sangria daily at Cha Cha Cha. We make more sangria than any restaurant in San Francisco, most nights selling enough to float a ship. No Cha Cha Cha meal feels right without sangria, but a glass of sangria, we believe, is also important to the cooking process. Put on some island music, pour a cool glass of sangria (keep in mind, we said one glass!), break out the chips and salsa, and start cooking.

1 orange, cut into ⅛-inch slices

1 lemon

1 cup sugar

1 bottle dry white wine

1 bottle dry red wine

Sliced peaches, grapes, strawberries, or other seasonal fruit (optional)

Gin, Grand Marnier, or brandy to taste (optional)

Combine the orange, lemon, sugar, and wines in a large glass bowl and stir for several minutes. Cover and refrigerate for at least 4 to 6 hours, or overnight. Add the optional fruits and spirits, if you like. Serve over ice or, just before serving, place some ice cubes in the punch bowl.

A Cha Cha Cha Discography and Bibliography

Africando, *Tierra Tradicional* (Sterns, 1045).

Coupé Cloué, *36 Ans Aprés* (MMI Records, MMI CD 1030).

Cortijo y Kako y Sus Tamores, *Ritmos y Cantos Callejeros* (Ansonia, HGCD 1477).

Cortijo y Su Combo, *Baile con Cortijo y Su Combo con Ismael Rivera* (Seeco Tropical, 90513).

LoKassa et Soukous Stars, *LoKassa et Soukous Stars* (Syllar Productions, SYLCD 83100).

Sam Mangwana, *No Me Digas No* (Blue Silver Distribution, 50-396-2).

Monguito, *Lo Mejor de Monguito, Volume 1* (SAR Records, SCD 1002).

Orchestra Rythmo Africa-Cubana, *Volume 1* (Tkios Musique, 779).

Orquestra Afro-Charanga, *Volume 2* (Thiokis Records, J521480).

Gnonnas Pedro, *La Compilation Musique Afro-Cubaine* (LeDoux Records, 79556-2).

Mon Rivera y Su Orquesta, *Karacatis Ki, Volume 1* (Ansonia Records, SALP 1356).

Nico Saquito, *Goodbye Mr. Cat* (World Circuit, 035).

Timbalada, *Timbalada* (Philips/Polygram, 314-518-068-2).

The following recordings are compilations by various artists:

Cuban Gold 2: Bajo con Tumbao (Qbadisc, QB9016).

Estrellas de Areito (Cuba Libre, 79902-2).

Exitos Mag (Discos Mag, 1267).

Guajira y Son Varios: The Real Cuban Music Series (Panart Records, 5165).

Noche Cubana, La Mejor de la Musica Cubana (Cuba Discos SA, CD No. 001).

The Original Mambo Kings, An Introduction to Afro-Cubop, 1948–1954 (Verve, 314-513-876-2-0510).

A Taste of the Indestructible Beat of Soweto (Earthworks 7243-839183-2).

While Santería is a thoroughly Cuban religion and culture, all of its sacred ceremonies, chants, and songs are still conducted in the Yoruba language. To better understand these songs and chants, and to further your understanding of the African influence on Cuban music, we recommend *Sacred Rhythms of Cuban Santería*, Smithsonian Folkways (SF CD 40419).

Reliable sources for Cuban and Afro-Cuban music:

Round World By Mail
593 Guerrero Sreet
San Francisco, CA 94110
(415) 255-7384

Green Linnet Records, Inc.
43 Beaver Brook Road
Danbury, CT 06810
(203) 730-0333

QBADISC
P.O. Box 1256
Old Chelsea Station
New York, NY 10011
(212) 620-0320

To learn more about Santería, we recommend the following books:

González-Wippler, Migene. *Legends of Santería*. St Paul: Llewellyn Publications, 1994.

———. *Santería: The Religion*. St. Paul: Llewellyn Publications, 1994.

Murphy, Joseph M. *Santería: African Spirits in America*. Boston: Beacon Press, 1993.

Glossary of Terms and Techniques

A

achiote paste: Made from brick red annatto seeds, and often used as a natural food coloring, achiote paste is acidic and orange-scented. The paste is used in Latino sauces and marinades.

almonds, toasting: Spread the almonds evenly on a baking sheet and bake in a preheated 350°F oven for 5 to 7 minutes, or until the almonds turn a light golden brown.

annatto oil: In a medium saucepan, combine 1 cup vegetable oil and ½ cup annatto seeds. Cook over medium heat, stirring occasionally, until the liquid has turned orange. Let cool and strain through a sieve. Store in an airtight jar in the refrigerator indefinitely.

B

bijol: A blend of ground annatto seed, corn flour, and ground cumin, often used to give rice a saffron color in lieu of the more expensive saffron threads.

C

canola oil: A mild vegetable oil readily available in most large grocery stores.

cascabel chilies: Dark reddish brown dried round chilies about 2 inches in diameter. Very hot.

chipotle chilies: Smoked dried jalapeño chilies, available dried or in adobo sauce in cans.

cilantro: A tangy green herb, also known as fresh coriander and Chinese parsley.

clarified butter: In a saucepan melt butter over low heat. Gently pour off the clear top layer of clarified butter, discarding the milky residue.

coconut, toasting: Spread coconut flakes or shreds evenly on a baking sheet and bake in a preheated 350°F for 4 to 7 minutes, or until lightly browned.

coconut milk: A sweet, thick milk made from coconut flesh, available canned or frozen in the international food sections of most markets.

crab boil: A spice used for boiled crab and gumbo, easily found in most large grocery stores.

F

filé powder: Ground dried sassafras leaves used to flavor and thicken gumbo; readily available.

G

ginger, fresh: This tropical rhizome is used in making ginger beer and in many Asian cuisines. Peel before using, and cut the slices as thin as possible.

guava paste: A thick paste made from the sweet pink flesh of the guava, available at specialty foods shops.

H

habanero chilies: Indigenous to Cuba, these small, orange, lantern-shaped chilies are named after that nation's capital. Available fresh and dried, they must be seeded before using. These chilies are very hot and great care must be used when cooking with them. Plastic gloves should always be used when handling the chilies. Take care not to touch your eyes or sensitive skin. Wash your gloves and cooking implements in hot soapy water after handling the chilies. Red pepper flakes are the most common substitute for these chilies.

hoisin sauce: A sweet, dark, spicy ketchuplike condiment, available in most international food sections and at Asian groceries.

J

jalapeño-flavored vinegar: Commercially bottled vinegar flavored with bits of jalapeño. Available at most gourmet shops.

jalapeño jack cheese: A Monterey Jack cheese with bits of jalapeños in it, a lovely combination of cool and hot.

jalapeños: These small fresh green chilies range from hot to very hot, and should always be seeded before using in any dish. They are perhaps the most peppery of all the chilies.

juniper berries: Available fresh or dried, these small green berries are almost always ground before using.

L

lizano: A tangy, turmeric-based marinade from Costa Rica, used to marinate fish and beef. It is available in specialty foods shops and Latino groceries.

M

Monterey Jack cheese: A mild California cheese that is commonly used in Mexican dishes to replace Mexican cheeses not widely available here.

N

negro chilies: see pasilla chilies.

New Mexico chilies: Long, mild chilies, available both fresh or dried in either green or red. Often called Anaheim chilies.

P

pasilla chilies: Dried chilaca chilies. *Pasilla* is Spanish for "little raisin," and these dark brown chilies smell faintly of raisins. In some parts of California and Mexico, fresh poblanos and anchos (dried poblanos) are mistakenly called pasillas. Mild to hot.

pasilla powder: Ground pasilla chilies.

plantains: A member of the banana family, plantains must be cooked. The skins are almost completely black when the plantains are ripe.

polenta: Coarsely ground cornmeal.

pumpkin seeds, toasting: In a dry skillet over medium heat, toast pumpkin seeds, stirring occasionally, for 2 to 3 minutes, or until lightly browned.

R

rice wine vinegar: Japanese vinegar, available plain or seasoned with sugar and salt.

S

Scotch bonnet chili: Closely related to the habanero chili and similar in appearance, though smaller, this small, round, wrinkled chili is very hot and comes in yellow, orange, or red. Use rubber gloves when handling it and take care not to touch your eyes or sensitive skin. Wash the gloves and all cooking implements in hot soapy water after handling this chili.

sesame seeds, toasting: In a dry skillet over medium-low heat, toast sesame seeds, stirring occasionally, for 1 or 2 minutes, or until lightly browned.

shrimp, peeling and deveining: Peel the shell and legs and discard. With a small sharp knife, cut slightly into the outer curve of the shrimp; remove and discard the dark vein.

squid, cleaning: Rinse the squid and separate the head (in the center) and tentacles from the body. Remove the ink sac and discard. Separate the tentacles from the head, discarding the head. Squeeze the hard round beak out of the tentacles. Remove the long quill inside the body. Rinse the body and tentacles under cold running water and drain well. Cut the body into ½-inch rings.

T

tamarind juice: The sweet juice of the tamarind pod, available canned at most Latino groceries.

toasted sesame oil: A dark, highly flavored oil available in many supermarkets and Asian markets.

tomatillos: Small green tart vegetables that look like tomatoes with a papery husk. Always remove the husk before rinsing or using.

tomatoes, peeling and seeding: Immerse tomatoes in a pot of boiling water for 30 seconds to 1 minute. Using a slotted spoon, transfer the tomatoes to a bowl of cold water. Remove the skin. Cut the tomatoes in half, hold them upside down over the sink, and squeeze out the seeds.

tortillas, toasting: Put tortillas on a baking sheet and toast in a preheated 300°F oven for 5 to 7 minutes, or until golden brown.

Acknowledgments

Whether it was Russ whipping our famous floral table-cloths out from under a fully set and occupied table, Nancy designing and hand painting our first T-shirt, or Tina taking a surprised customer for a quick dance in the aisles, the floor staff at Cha Cha Cha has always been a uniquely talented group. They've not only dealt with the slow and busy times with great aplomb, but they've exhibited a host of other gifts and talents, from Nancy and Lee belting out bluesy rock and roll with David Doucet on bass, to Mark Takai giving dance lessons at our infamous warehouse Christmas party.

Our staff has been like the dawn patrol of the dining room: tough (it is Haight Street, after all), brave (at least with a cup of sangría hidden under the counter), and loyal (especially at the end of the month). In a small city crowded with over three thousand restaurants, one could only hope for a staff that included Lee Shupp, Monica Bosson, Daniel César, Jala Pradham, Nancy Terzian, Kristina and Gretchen Schubeck, and what seemed like the whole Navaratte family.

It was always fun watching our customers' perplexed and curious faces as they passed through our kitchen. What were all those pink-scrubbed Irish faces doing in a Caribbean restaurant on Haight Street in San Francisco? What, indeed! For a while it seemed the heart of Cha Cha Cha rested on the ol' sod, and you can believe that many a beer (I mean sangría) was hoisted after a shift by Mars Buckley, John Meany, Maebh O'Byrne, and Catherine O'Neill. But I'm sure they didn't have to tug too strongly on the sleeves of David Sanfield, Patty Stirling, Vinnie Wright, and Paul Robben to join them. Those Irish! These were followed by a few of lesser appetite, but not skill: Christine Oncken, Andrew Gillen, Juan Morales, Adolfo Juarez, Jose Rodriguez, and Max Reynosa. And of course, those stalwarts in the back of the house: Rambo, Salvador Clares, and Salvado Rodriguez.

Special thanks to:

Russ Hahn, general manager, who all these many years has really been the focal point of the restaurant. That he genuinely treats customers as friends has turned many a first-time customer into a regular.

Bill Higgins, executive chef, without whose yeomanlike devotion in tasting, writing, and editing these recipes, this book would never have happened.

Carmen Garcia, assistant manager, for her verve, style, and pluckiness. She keeps us on course, and has added much to the Cha Cha Cha look, which can be seen in her altar to Ochosi. And yes, Carmen, we will put mofongo on the menu.

Gabriela Salas, who with her constant trips to her native Costa Rica (in mind and body) kept us supplied with a never-ending stream of local dishes. A truly gifted chef, she always pushed the boundaries, and often showed up with bags of exotic foods from local Asian markets, which would later reappear in startling and wonderful combinations with our own Caribbean staples.

A very special thanks to the late Jimmy Harris, who not only talked himself into a job at Cha Cha Cha, but cooked us into Bea Pixa's *San Francisco Chronicle* column, a milestone for which he will always be remembered.

And to the Santeros, Miguel Angel Garcia, Patrick Omi Eleke Egry, and Ruben Texidar, thanks again for the altars.

Lastly, and probably most importantly, we were fortunate to open Cha Cha Cha where we lived, the curious Haight-Ashbury district of San Francisco. Not known for their conservatism, the inhabitants of this unique neighborhood allowed us to make mistakes, to be a little wacky, a little offbeat; they've admired our altars, enjoyed our food, and joined us in having a good time. And thanks, Debra, Dick, and Charles.

Recipe Index